# Nights of a Taxi

## Introduction Nights of a Taxi Driver

## Introduction

About me and how I started.

### Ricky's Taxi Stories.

Takeaways Explained.

This Happen in One Night.

What a Night !!!!!.

Some times you say the wrong thing.

Road Rage !!!.

This Happened with One Fare !!

_____-****_____

This is all you need to be a taxi driver.

**Patience**
**Calm**
**Honest**
**Having a Sense of Humour**
**Being Understanding**

_____-****_____

## Plus……

## Tim's Taxi Stories

_____-****_____

Hi,

My name is Ricky and here is my book on funny taxi stories that has happen to me over the years, there are 3 in the series and I decided to put them all in one paperback book, it all started when a friend suggested why don't you try working as a part time taxi driver, I thought what a great idea, meet people and get paid for it, so within 3 weeks I'd passed my taxi tests got my badge and have been working with the same company for over 15 years, I never thought in a million years I would have so much to say about the times I drove a taxi and my first fare??

Well, I had to pick up from Dove Tale Close in Ilfracombe and guess what!!!!!........they never turned up, what a start I thought but soon over the years stories started to come in, at first I didn't think much about it but then started to write them down, soon I thought is it me or am I just unlucky.

So after all these years I finally got the stories published for all to see hope you all like them.

Ricky


# Night of a Taxi Driver

During my years of being a taxi driver in Ilfracombe North Devon, I've had my fair share of funny people and not so nice people, good and bad jobs, and since being a taxi driver, I've delivered (Not all at once)...... Front Door Keys, Bag of Clothes, Nappies, Cigarettes, Sweets, Milk, Bag of Sugar, Milky Bars, Chocolate Digestives Biscuit's, Wine, Beer, Gin, a Jumper, 24 Pizzas at once, Cat Food, Dog Biscuits, Fish Tank, Flat Screen TV, 2 Bicycles, 6 Large Boxes of Frozen Chips & Money.

I've also had Newly Weds, Bridesmaids, People dressed as Frankenstein, Batman and Robin, Spiderman, Wizards, Witches, Fairies, Werewolf, Pirates, Bumble Bee, Cowboys and characters from Beatrix's Potter in the taxi and I've seen some very funny things and here are some I would like to share with you…………..**believe it or not these are <u>all</u> true stories……….**

## Ricky's Taxi Stories

Picked up a guy off the rank wanting to go to Wilder Road, he sat in the back and quite drunk, so off we go, goes down to the bottom of Northfield Road in Ilfracombe and I say which way mate ?? He said take a left so I did, got to the top of Wilder Road …nothing….turned around at the War Memorial and went back down Wilder Road he says keep driving, carried on down to the bottom ( which is about one mile) I'm still asking where to mate ????....... but no response, so turned around by the Waverley and up Ropery Road then up Wilder Road again, he said keep driving I will pay you……..so I did!!…he says go faster, but I told him there was a police car behind me (There wasn't) so I can't… well, I'm still asking where to mate and after going down and up Wilder Road 6 times….yes 6 times !!!!!..... we eventually end up at the top of Wilder Road, pulled over by Jack's Dairy and he staggers out the back of the cab and goes inside leaving the front door wide open….I waited a few minutes and his wife comes storming out shouting where have you been with my husband !!!!!……..me ??…..I said……he wouldn't tell me where he lived !!…..how much is this going to cost me ??……..still shouting…….well ….the meter was running, so I got her to pay that she wasn't very happy but paid it……then the other taxi driver I was working with asked where have you been ??……he couldn't stop laughing when I told him, Fare should have taken 3 minutes but ended up being 25minutes.

Funny thing happened while I was sitting on the rank in number 2 position, a guy looking worse for wear walked up to the first taxi and tried to open the front door, he missed the handle and slid down the side of the taxi and got wedged between the taxi and the kerb, his one leg showing , waving around frantically trying to get up, with his leg high in the air, the taxi driver got out after a few minutes and looking at me gestured where is he ??........me crying with laughter pointed to the guy down the other side of the cab with his leg still shaking trying to un-wedge himself, he finally got him up and into the cab, the cab driver shaking his head in disbelief and still I'm laughing.

One day I picked up a couple who had just got married that day and they wanted a taxi to Narracott Grand Hotel Woolacombe, still in her wedding dress, him still in his suite.....took them down there and gave them a cut price fare......
Like you do, anyway went straight back to Ilfracombe and done 2 more taxi jobs, sitting on the rank I noticed £30 on the back seat, thinking the last people to sit there was the wedding couple, as it was their first night after the wedding I thought I'd wait until the morning, so I phoned up the Narracott and told them that I found some money on the back seat could they contact them in the Honeymoon suite and tell them.... I left my phone number and waited......nothing, thinking that I might have caused their first row ,I phoned again......they had gone...so I spent the money on 3 bottles of wine at our Xmas taxi do.

Guy phones up wanting a taxi from the High street, picks him up and all his mates are having a go at him………not surprised really………my shortest trip ……100 yards……….Chocolate Box High Street to Ketch up Portland Street @ 1.0am so £3.50.

Picked up a girl off the taxi rank just after midnight and took her to Queens Avenue, forgot to put the meter on and when we got there she started to kick off saying I'm not paying that fare !!!!!, it's robbery, other taxi firms don't charge that much, I'm not drunk enough for you to over charge me !!!…. etc… etc…after 5mins she calmed down………….after, I told her that the meter was displaying the time 12.50 not the fare…………lol.

Picked up off the rank going to Combe Martin, on the way there the guys asked how much it will cost, well the meter was running, so I said about £12 give or take a few pounds, that was not what they thought it would be, so for the next 10mins all I got was….. can you give us a discount ??........other taxi firms charge less !!............how far would £10 take us…..just to name a few……….so where do want to be dropped off ??….. I said ….coming down into

Combe Martin……..Oh ….on the seafront, where are you going I replied ….Oh…the Castle Inn they said………well the meter was saying about £10, so I said ….I can take you there if you want…………no ….it's ok, so I dropped them off at the seafront……..they gave me £10…..plus a £2 tip…………….is there any logic in that !!!!!!!!!!!

Had a call to pick up a guy from the Bunch of Grapes, got outside and waited for him to come out…..a few minutes later he appears…..so where are you going mate…..a few seconds later …Hele he says in a drunken voice…….and you are late !!….. sorry mate, I only just got the call ,he mutters something…….so I'm facing the wrong way and there's no cars coming up the high street so I did a quick 3 point turn….he turns to me and says…..I don't like your attitude….what !!!!…. I said, I don't like your attitude he says again….sorry mate…nothing wrong with my attitude I said……I'm thinking there's loads wrong with his !!!…..anyway off we go…..meter on…… he's still complaining about my attitude…..ok, going down into Hele……where do you want to be dropped off ?....I said…..there's a delay then he says….over there outside Hillbillies……ok I said……stops and the meter says £4.35, so I said just give me £4.00….I'm not paying that he says ….as you have got a bad attitude…..now I'm starting to get fed up with this guy….so I said, come on mate just pay the money and I will get on my way…….he gets his hand in his pocket and pulls out some change and a load more money comes flying out as he pulls his hand out of his pocket and goes all over the floor of the taxi….he gives me £3.00 and says I'm not paying anymore !!….staggers out of the taxi……slams the door and walks down the road………looking down on the floor of the taxi must be about £8.00 in loose change or more…..so for my attitude….I through that was a nice tip he gave me !!!!!

Picked up some guys from the Ship & Pilot going to Dove Tail Close, the old guy in the front for some reason or other started to pick on me, do you know where Dove Tail Close is he says??......Yes, I do I said…….. you are not local are you he says?……...I said yes ….am afraid I am…you don't sound local he said….what's your name he said……Ricky, I said…..no your last name he said……Teeling, I said…….my name is one of the oldest names in Ilfracombe he says…..is it I said…

so is mine I said (Thinking I shouldn't of said that !!!!)…boy this guy is now starting to annoy me!!!!...........how old is your name ??….I don't know but my gran and granddad use to own Larkstone café years ago…..never heard of them he says in a grumpy voice……..well, they did I said……..*by the way all this time he was giving me directions to Dove Tail Close!!*...........we get to Dove Tail Close and he says to me……( while paying me ) that was the worse taxi ride he has ever had and he won't be using us again……..thank god for that I said…..and he slams the door and storms off.

## Takeaways Explained

Takeaways now days are part of our job, some taxi firms do it, but some don't (It saves sitting on the taxi rank doing and earning nothing) this is to explain what happens……… starts off with a person phoning up a takeaway shop and ordering what they want and leaving their name, address & phone number, then they or the takeaway shop phones us up to collect it, we pay for it (but sometimes it's more money than we have, so we collect the money owed and bring it back to the takeaway shop)……(it doesn't always work out like that)!!!!!!….. then the person pays us for the takeaway and the delivery charge (depends where it's going)……see easy or is it ????

## This happened in one night !!!!

1.
Food order from Asian Spice going to Woolacombe Bay Holiday Park with a phone number attached to contact them, arrived at the holiday park, phoned lady to say I'm in reception....waited....and ...waited....phoned again asked where she is, she said she is on her way........waited.......phoned again 5 mins later, she says she is in the reception at Woolacombe Bay Holiday Park, I tell her she can't be as I'm here and nobody else is.....so asked her again where are you, she still said she was at Woolacombe Bay Holiday Park......ok, me thinks she is at Woolacombe Bay Hotel so drives down there (about a mile) and no one is there, phoned again, she still said she is still in Woolacombe Bay Holiday Park reception, so I said look you can't be please ask the reception where you are...........( yes, I thought to myself, she

is a blonde ....no doubt ).........seconds later...O yes she said I was reading the Woolacombe Bay Holiday advertising Board opposite me.................and guess what !!!!!!!!!!!!!!!!!...........................She is at GOLDEN COAST HOLIDAY PARK !!!!!!!!!!!!!!!!!!!! 2 miles away........and when I get there......she's a blonde.......I told you.

2.
Food order from Asian Spice going to Woolacombe Bay Holiday Park again !!! This time phoned her from Asian Spice to check she is where she said she is, arrive at holiday park phoned lady to say I'm in reception....waited....and waited....phoned again after waiting 5 more minutes asked where she is, she says she is sending down her 2 sons to pick it up and they are driving a blue Mazda.......waited........waited.......phoned again, she said they left 10 mins ago...........waited.....in the end I phoned her to see where she really is......................Woolacombe Bay Hotel Apartments !!!!!!!.....next to Woolacombe Bay Hotel...........one and a half hours to deliver 2 food orders !!!!!!

In the meantime my pick up from Ilfracombe Bus station says she will be 15 mins early......so Woolacombe to Ilfracombe in record time !!!!!!

3.
 Picked up a little old lady at Ilfracombe bus station going to Mortehoe near Woolacombe, earlier on the phone she asks me have I got 2 screwdrivers as she has left her suitcase keys at home in Colchester, sorry madam I said, we don't carry things like that in the taxi, anyway picked this lovely old lady up and find that her sister in-law has a garage, so on arrival at Mortehoe ( with the taxi phone going 10 to a dozen ) I proceed to the garage and with luck find a junior hack saw...............yippee .........so went back to the house and with 2 little old ladies looking over my shoulder I proceed to cut off the lock, with mind your fingers ringing in my ear and what a clever man he is............taxi phone is still ringing ........got a £5 tip for my troubles.

4.
So can the night get any stranger......or worse............you bet !!!!!..................Phone call,

can you pick up from Buddies going to Oxford park, arrives on time and in seconds a lady gets in the back absolutely hammered, gets to Oxford Park………..I got no money....she says she will have to go inside and get some..........trouble is the front door has a coded key lock, so me watching this pissed up woman wobbling all over the place..........note !! **not** a lady anymore !!.........trying to get in through the front door........after 5 mins I decided to help her, out the cab I get.........so what's the number ???? ….. she says...........3....4.....4.....5.....6....ok...........done that.....nothing.....won't open......... so what's the number I say....again !!!.......
3....4.....4.....5.....6....ok...........done that.....nothing.....won't open........again..........so what's the number I said again......guess what it's different...........3....4.....5.....6....ok...........done that.........nothing.........won't open……in the mean time I stopped her falling into the bushes…...she starts shouting up at the window and everyone looked out the window.......................except the one person she was shouting at...........anyway someone came down and let her in...........now I'm thinking.....am I going to get paid??...........the

answer is yes !!!!...........seconds later door opens and I get paid...........by someone else.

At the time all this was quite stressful, and thought this could only happen to me, but looking back even through not one of the food orders gave me a tip, but at least I got a £5 tip from a lovely old Lady.

# What a night !!!!!!!!

Had a pick up from The Little Mermaid pub, pouring with rain and guess who ??.......Reg !!!!!, now this guy I've never seen sober, his every other word begins with F*** and when he's drunk he's bad tempered with it, also he has a pair of crutches, so you can imagine what state he comes out of the pub at, anyway I'm parked outside and his mate come out first and gets in the back, next Reg comes out looking worse for wear when he misses the car door handle and slides down the side of car into the gutter. ( Note still pouring with rain ).

Well, I waited a few minutes and the people sitting next to the window of the pub was looking down at him, so I thought I would get out and help him as his mate wouldn't. As I get around to his side of the taxi, there he is, flat out in the gutter with the water going up his trouser leg and coming out of his shirt collar, the landlord came out and I said you got him in this state, so you can look after him. His mate finally got out and carried him inside.

Well, thinking that was it, 30-40mins later another call to pick someone up at the Little Mermaid......yes, you guessed it......Reg !!!!, this time he got in the taxi ( With his mate ) and off we go, stops outside his front door he pays then he gets out walks few steps then trips up and head butts the door, by this time he's swearing ten to a dozen and his mate helps him up, he looked ok, so I left them to it as they walk through the front door.

Had to pick up 7 girls in the Square in Barnstaple at 2.00am, waited for about 15mins and one at a time they would appear, got to about number 5 when one of the girls said.........sorry we are late here is a burger and chips, so I thought that was a nice gesture, so I said, look I can't drive and eat this do you mind if I sit in the back with you ???...... no they said, so there's me sitting in the back of the bus at 2.30am with 7 lovely girls all eating burger & chips having a right old laugh, anyway time to go home, so off I drive with the radio on full with them singing and laughing………..when I dropped them off in Ilfracombe they said it was the best taxi ride ever !!!!!!!!

Picked up a couple off the rank wanting to go to Fern Way, guy has just brought a pizza, so get to Fern Way and I think the guy was thinking it was his lucky night, as he said what are you up to now ?? and the girl said well, I'm going home pays the taxi fare gets out and leaves him sitting all alone in the back of the taxi, so mate where do you want to go ??.......back to the rank he says but I got no money, that's fine I says………2 slices of pizza should do it, so gets to the rank and he pays with the pizza's………boy….. was I hungry……lol. One night got called to Chickenland to pick someone up, pulled up outside and on the pavement was this guy flat out and sick all down him………a guy comes running up to me saying can you take this guy home……sorry mate not in that state !!.......I'll give you £40 if you do, he says…….forget it mate, I would't do it for £140 … and drove off………later I see these guys walking along the high street falling all over the place….at least I had clean seat covers.

One Saturday night I had the phone in the taxi, we were very busy and I was giving out other jobs to the drivers, I picked up a family wanting to go from the High Street up to the Rugby Club, the 2 kids were a bit lively and moving around in the back of the taxi even though I told them to button up and calm down. Arrives at the Rugby Club and pulls over and the phone starts ringing. I answer it, but I can't hear a thing as the kids were yelling and making a racket I told the parents if they could keep them quiet but no joy !!  So, still can't hear what the people on the phone were saying as the kids were screaming, so I turned around and told them to be quiet, that didn't go down well with the parents they paid me and stormed off………………………thinking that was the end of it. I later gave the phone to the other driver and he sent me to pick up some people from the Rugby Club………yep you guessed it !!….it was them again, the woman got in the front and from the Rugby Club to the High Street she tore into me......How dare you shout at my kids !!!....I am reporting you to your boss !!!!....I will have your badge for this !!!!.....and so on and so on, I tried keeping my cool and nearly did but when they started swearing at me that was it !!!!! I told them if they didn't stop swearing I would stop the taxi and they can walk home.....that made them even worse.......finally got to the High Street and after a few exchanges which seemed to last a life time… I got the taxi fare......and they finally got out...... and slammed the door.

Pick up 8 people in the mini bus coming from Combe Martin to Ilfracombe seafront….meter on, gets to Sandpiper and checked the meter £24, took £2 off and charged them £22, thinking that was ok………..nope the guy in the front seat thought I was ripping him off and started to go off on one !!.......why does this cost so much?? He said, I tried to explain to him that I don't set the prices. That's what the meter said and I've taken £2 off as well…..still he was going on refusing to pay the fare and telling me he was going on the internet to complain about North Devon Taxi prices he wanted my badge number, so I gave him that and also the phone number of the North Devon Council I gave him that….still he wasn't happy….meter now read £26 and I told him if he doesn't pay now that on the meter is what he has to pay…….still no joy, radioed to boss what was happening, he arrived minutes later and he told him the same as me, still he's going on one, his wife said to him to pay it, no.. he wasn't going to back down, police arrived and when he saw them he quickly paid up muttering that we were a bunch of thieves and stormed off ……………never heard anything after that.

I carry a small pocket torch now and here's why……..One night I picked up a food order from Bombay Palace going to Furze Hill Road, arrived at the address and started walking up the path towards the house it was very quiet …..I couldn't see a thing it was that dark, all of a sudden I tripped up over a step and landed on the ground…..the quietness was soon gone with a loud crunch of the Popper domes as I hit the ground, got up brushed myself down and went to the house and knocked on the door.

A few minutes later the door open by about 2 inches and a person looked through the gap in the door and asked how much did I want ??.........I told her how much and was just about to explain what happened down on the path when the door slammed shut......seconds later a hand came out with the money, gap in the door was about 3 inches now and another hand came out and grabbed the food order then the door slammed shut again !!!!......walked slowly down the path in the dark, not knowing where the step was, I must have looked pretty silly doing a ministry of funny walks, trying to find the step I tripped up on, got to the bottom of the path and off home to change as I had mud all over my jeans....

Ok, Nearly time to go home when a guy wants a taxi to Meadow Farm.......never heard of Meadow Farm so needed assistance from the guy when I pick him up, guy gets in looked a bit drunk but he said he has a very good idea where it is, so with the meter running we leaving Buddy's going along towards St Brannock's Road and yes, he remembers going up that road, then he sees another landmark and yes, we are on the right road he says, going up towards Mullacott and all seems to be ok……..until we reach the top and he says…..can't remember this, are you sure I said, yes, this isn't it, so about turn and head back down Mullacott to Buddy's with the meter still running.

Ok, I said, can you give me a clue of what you saw when you walked into town this morning, seconds later, well I remember the swimming baths, hah ha I thought, that's on the way to Hele now we are getting somewhere, by this time people are phoning up wondering where there taxi is, but on we went, passed the swimming baths so still thinking where on earth is Meadow Farm, then for some reason I said it's not Little Meadow is it ?????

Yes, that's it he says excitingly…. so off we go……… more phone calls wanting a taxi, gets to Little Meadow and then the fun starts…turned around at the entrance …meter read £28.00 I took £8.00 off, as he looked annoyed it was that price, they said it would only cost £10 he says, I said it would of if you didn't take me half way to Braunton, anyway he finally got the idea that I wanted £20 so he threw it at me and slammed the car door. Finally picked up the people who phoned me asking where is my taxi………………20mins late.

Picked up a girl and she wanted me to pick her friend up as she was running late, waited outside her friends house for a few minutes and she came down the steps holding her clothes and carrier bags, she gets in and off we go to the High street, looked like they were having a sleep over, they paid the taxi fare and started to get out leaving a sanitary towel on the back seat as she started to close the taxi back door I told her would she mind if she could take all her stuff, both girls looked at each other and gave a almighty scream went red in the face and grabbed the towel heard them laughing as they walk down the road.

Came back to Ilfracombe and got told to go to the Millennium Chicken by Jessica, to pick up a food order going to 8 Horne Park Road…………She thinks !!........mmmm me thinks this going to be a funny one, so picked up the food order and off I go to 8 Horne Park Road, gets there and finds No. 6 so working my way up the road Hah ha….No.7, pulls outside the next house thinking it's No. 8 and apart that there's a dog barking at the window….no answer….waited a few minutes… knocked again …..nothing (Dog still barking)

So since there was no number on the door or gate I drove to the next house…..yes, you guessed it, it had No.8 on the door, went down a path knocked on the door, a few minutes later an old guy open opened the door looking quite bemused, Did you order a Chinese takeaway ??....I said……..No, he said and promptly shuts the door.

Ok, back to what Jessica said No.8 …I think!!!.......I drove to No.9……..Yippee….That's the address, certainly glad to get rid of the food order as it was starting to get cold.


Had a taxi job to pick up a lady from Tiverton Parkway to New Beginnings (Health Spa), picked her up and started talking to each other about life and trying to put the world to right……as you do !!!! found out she is a film director call Judith Ann Hunt, who knew everyone in the film industry ( She directed the Loch Ness monster film ) then eventually came to the reason why she is going to New Beginnings…..to detox and get away from work.

Well, on the way she started to talk about having one final drink of wine, and asked me if I would join her in a drink……sorry, I can't….. as I'm driving I said, anyway she still wanted that final drink so pulls over at Tesco's Barnstaple and it's a certain wine she required White Chardonnay but must be cold, found one but couldn't find any plastic cups to drink out of, so off to Tesco's in Ilfracombe…..found some plastic cups and pulled over in the Tesco's car park and open the wine for her, poured the wine and sat in the car park looking over Ilfracombe, New Beginnings phone asking where is she ??…..just coming out of Barnstaple she says……..anyway she finished her last plastic cup of wine and I took her to New Beginnings…. she gave me the wine which was left over, the plastic cups & £20 tip…………not bad heh !!


Picked a guy up off the rank at 1.00am and he wanted to go home, when we got there I found out he had no money, well me being a guy who sticks to his guns ….I said that's ok………and duly took him back to the taxi rank and told him to get out of the cab…..sorry I don't do freebies, I said…..and told the rest of the taxi drivers that this guy has no money………….the guy had to walk home…… shame !!!!!

 Phone in the taxi rings……can I have a taxi please………of course you can…..where are you and where do you want to go ??............we are on the pier and we want to go to ???????.......sorry I don't know that address……can you tell me where about it is ??………anyway ,she's trying to tell me where it is and I thought that's not in Ilfracombe……where are you phoning from…… Weston Super Mare she replies…..sorry love…… but I would love to pick you up but it would take me a few hours to get there…………..there was a festival going on that day in Weston Super Mare and one of our taxi's had to go and pick someone up from there……….and this lady saw the phone number on the side of the taxi thinking we were a local taxi company.


Picked up a couple from Woolacombe going to Ilfracombe, gets in the taxi and they changed their minds and wanted to go to Barnstaple instead, she was so drunk she couldn't  stand, he helped her in and she promptly fell asleep.

Had a chat with the guy for about 3 miles told him it would be about £30 but put the meter on just in case, he says she's got the money…….. and he fell asleep minutes later.

Arrived in Barnstaple and the old alarm bells start going, so pulls over and wakes him up asks him where do they want to be dropped off…..he says Forches Estate now the bells are ringing louder, so I asked him for the £30 before I take them there. He says she has it, but still she is in the land of Nod, so he said can you take me to a cash point (Tesco's) he gets out leaves her still fast asleep on the back seat comes back pays me £30…..great got my money.

He says, can I take him somewhere close to Forches, no problem it's on my way home but if you want I will take you there for £3.50, he declines, can you drop us off on the roundabout opposite Taw garages ………..Yep, no problem, pulls over and yes she is still fast asleep, so he has to drag her out of the cab, her skirt up around her neck showing everything and then her trainers catch something and flick off, so there she is…. fast asleep still, showing her knickers and tights to passing motorists and her trainers gone in all directions standing in a puddle of water, him saying ' I don't believe this' frantically holding on to her for dear life………he shuts the door……and I'm gone !!!!!!...bet he wished he'd taken me up on the lift home………lol.

Ok, got told to go to Lee to pick up some people……….yes, by Jessica again !!!……she writes down where the pickup is…. Park Cottage…….

**The instructions**……

Go pass Lincombe Cross going into Lee Bay, <u>**before**</u> you get to the Lee Bay sign there is a sharp corner, don't go around the corner go straight on, go down the road and the cottage is on the right clearly marked Park Cottage, next to a grey cottage… so, off I go……………gets there and down the road I go…….On the right….nothing……carries on down the road and it divides into 2 up right  towards 2 cottages or down left to some more…….so right I go, got outside the cottages and no it's not it, turns around as it's a dead end…….down the road towards the others and end up in a farm yard, turns around again and headed back up to where I started on the main road.

Phoned Jessica to let her know that I can't find it, spots a women walking her dog so asked her where Park Cottage is …….not around here she says…..go down the road **pass** the Lee Bay sign and go around a sharp corner and it's on your right….gets there on time, waited for about 5 mins one person came out and said they will be a couple of minutes….noticed one of them watering the garden…..and he could see me waiting….finally he got in and off to Ilfracombe I go.


Got a phone call and asked if I could take someone to a farm near Mortehoe, he was in the high street and when I got there he ( aged about 70 – 75 ) was being held up by a passer-by, The guy said I think he wants to go to Mortehoe, I found him on the floor in a shop door way, but can't understand him. Don't worry mate I know exactly where he lives Higher Slade, so off we go…….gets to the farm at higher Slade and he wouldn't let me take him up to his house, he paid the fare and opened the door, I booked the details in and when I looked up he was nowhere to be seen, I reversed back and there he was sitting in the hedge, I got out of the taxi and pulled him out

…..you ok ??....I asked, yeah fine he says, do you want me to take you up the road to your house ??….no he says. So, I straighten him up and went back to the taxi leaving him walking up the road, He then lost his balance and started to run backwards and fell over again, gets out the taxi again, he was clearly unstable on his feet, so went into a barn and found a large wooden broom, got him up off the floor, straighten him up again !!!!, gave him the broom he swayed and few times and the last I saw of him he was walking up the road in the dark with the broom in one hand walking all over the place.

Got a call to pick up at Barnstaple train station, arrived at the station and parks on the taxi rank……seconds later I'm surrounded by 3 - 4 taxi drivers……you can't park here they said…….sorry but it's a taxi rank….and believe it or not I'm in a taxi !!….you still can't park here they said,  But I'm waiting for a person who's coming in on the next train I said….you still can't park here they said, starting to get a bit angry…..ok, I will park over there outside the main entrance I said……..so drove over to the entrance and waited…..train came in and everybody wanted to get into my cab the taxi drivers were looking at me and if looks could kill I was dead in seconds…….lol….lucky the girl I was picking up came out and got in the taxi……I drove off knowing 4 pair of eyes was watching me with interest.

Picked up 3 scouser's off the rank wanting to go to Hele, half way there one of them says can we pay you tomorrow, sorry lads I'm not working tomorrow, noticed the one giving me all the grief is a guy who always complains about the fares, and I've had a few running's with him before……so I pulls over and said……look lads we have 3 options……number one ….I take you back to the taxi rank and drop you off……..Second option….We can drive to a cash machine but the meter will be running……Third option…..I can take you to Hele and one of you can go in and get some money…….the old boy who was sitting in the front seat persuaded me to take the third option and said the guy in the back has money at his house….so thinking it was the right thing to do I took them to Hele, 2 guys stayed in the taxi while the gobby one went inside and came out with the money…..plus a £1 tip…..see what us taxi drivers are up against !!!!!!


Number one on the rank late one night ,when a girl comes running around the corner racing up to the taxi and asking if I could pick up her friend around the corner……so, off I go around the corner and outside the night club, sitting on the floor with her legs wide open, totally off her head was a women who will remain anonymous as she might read this one day and this girl says can you take her home ??.......well I know in the past that this women will have no money…..and she sometimes wets herself……so I said no….sorry, just got a call to pick someone else up……..that was a close one !!!


Picked up a drunk from the Mermaid going to Oxford Grove, he gets in and wants to go to Jacks Dairy……….staggers out of the taxi and goes into the shop…..comes out with a 2 litre bottle of Cider, off we go to Oxford Grove and he starts to get out of the taxi and clinging for his dear life to the side of the taxi, I said…..hold on a minute mate, I will help you around the taxi…….to late…….he's gone……out of control, running down the road, falls after about 5 yards, I get hold of him with a help of another taxi driver and we get his front door keys and open the door…….gets him in and point him in the right direction towards the stairs…..then off we go and shut the front door.

Sitting on the rank at 10.55pm in the number 2 position when a guy passes the first taxi and gets in mine, he starts by saying ……..look I know it's sounds funny…..but I know it's £37.50 to Barnstaple on a Sunday would you do a return trip for £40….so me thinking well, I got to come back here anyway, so I said yes, I would….he gets in and says…….look I got £20 on me now but my money doesn't go in my bank account until 11.10pm, so can we go the Braunton way and pick my mate up and go to the bank there……….yep sounds good to me !!...........off we go….gets to Braunton at 11.10pm he goes to the hole in the wall……. nothing…….…..he tries again nothing……….waits until 11.15pm………nothing, looks like he is in panic stations !!!!..... he gets back in the taxi very worried, me thinking something is wrong ,so I said look…….give me your £20 now, let's go and pick your mate up and try getting your money out in Barnstaple……yes, he says that's a good idea, so off we go again. Gets to Barnstaple he gets his money out at last, I take him to this house, he comes out gives me the other £20 plus a £10 tip and we head back to Combe.

Picked up a guy going to Chambercombe, certainly had a lot to drink, I could just about understand where he wanted to go, pulls outside his house he pays and then falls out of the taxi, walks on all fours towards his gate, then starts talking to a cat…..wished I had a camera !!.......I turned the taxi around and passes him still talking to the cat…….I wonder if the cat could understand him more than me ??

**How desperate are people??……………and what cost??...........here are some examples…**

Lady phones and wants some Benson & Hedges cigarettes, goes to the shop in the high street, buys the cigarettes £5.60, takes them to Greenways fare £2.50, total price £8.10, delivers the cigarettes and she gives me a £10 and says keep the change…..talk about money to burn !!!!!!

Another phone call, different place Slade, wanting 20 Royals & 20 Benson & Hedges cigarettes, picks up cigarettes, dreading delivering them as I know what to expect……knocks on the door and the woman opens it, dressed in a dirty old dressing gown that looked like it had last month's dinner down it, not a pretty sight I can tell you!!!

Got a phone call with a request for 20 cigarettes & a box of cat biscuits, not just any old box of cat biscuits they had to be Tuna biscuit's, there's me looking for Tuna cat biscuit's in a shop in the high street, can't find any, but they had Tuna cat snacks and be totally honest I didn't know what the difference was…..so with the help of the shop assistant I brought them (2 packs), brought the cigarettes and off to Slade I go, knocks on the door and the girl was relieved I brought the Tuna snacks as the cat was really stressed out……not as stressed as me figuring out what biscuit's to buy a cat !!

Rollo…….now some of the taxi drivers will know his name, I picked up this guy many a time also delivered pizza's to his house, picking him up was always a problem as he was always drunk and couldn't stand for the life of him, many a time I would walk him to his door or watch him holding on to the wall slowly going to his front door, now talking about his door one day I was delivering a pizza to him, knocked on the door and he answered it, looking inside the house all I could see was newspaper and empty pizza boxes ( And I mean that is all you could see !!! ) they were everywhere on the floor, down the stairs over the furniture ……anyway I delivered the pizza and found out a month later he had fallen down the stairs tripping over a pizza box and broke his leg.

Most weekends I had a lovely job of picking up a nice old lady and taking her to Belmont Grange Residential Home, now you had to help her in and out the taxi, which was quite tricky sometimes especially if you are picking her up at Rainbow corner in the high street, anyway one night I picked her up at the Ship & Pilot and took her back

to Belmont Grange Residential Home, Wet &
blowing a gale that night.

Arrived outside and the first thing I would
do is ring the doorbell so the carers would know
we were outside, gets the lady out of the taxi and
still no carers so rings it again, minutes later a
young girl turns up with no shoes on and another
turns up and waits by the door, now we get the
lady up the front steps and the one by the door
doesn't lift a finger to help. There was some wheel
chair rams in the way so I said to her could she
help and move them out of the way.......with a
huff, she does it and we gets the lady up the front
steps and I leave them to it...........about 5
minutes later there's a phone call complaining
about the taxi driver (Me) who had just dropped
off a lady at Belmont Grange Residential Home,
sounded like the young girl who had no shoes on,
anyway she wanted to report me for my bad
attitude, I said that I would look into it (Knowing
that there was nothing wrong with my attitude) so I
reported myself...lol .......thinking maybe I
should do the same about her walking around with
no shoes on, think of all the germs she is spreading
!!!!

Phone rings….can I have a taxi please…yes love, where are you and where do you want to go ??……Well, I would like a taxi at 7.15pm from the Chinese takeaway in the high street to Princess Avenue……Ok…..that would be the Millennium Chicken going to Princess Avenue………no, I want the one from the high street………yes, Millennium Chicken is in the high street love……. No…. the one opposite the Welly………….yes, THAT is opposite the Welly…………she says so how long has it been called that ?????........since it has been open I think………ok….see you there in 10 minutes.

Sitting on the rank and the phone rings, hello there she says, I have only £8.00 and I was wondering how much a Veggie Burger would cost and how much the taxi fare would be ?..........Mmmmm that's a tough one I was thinking………..Have you phoned Maddy's chippy to fine out how much a Veggie Burger is ??  I said…. no I haven't she says………well, if you phone them and then phone me back, then I'll know if £8.00 is enough…..ok she says……….10 mins later she phones up and says it costs £2.30, so where do you live ??......Slade Valley she said……well that's about £4.00……silence for a few seconds (And you can hear her thinking I really want this burger) …….ok she says……….so one burger cost her £6.30…..and she gave me a tip.

 The Blue Dolphin restaurant phones…….can we have a taxi please, it's going to Mullacott Industrial Estate………..yes, I'm on my way…..gets down and there is a queue about 5 yards long waiting to be served Fish & Chips…… guy gets in and off we go……..on the way up he tells me that they have run out of chips…..we go in the estate and I waited outside a unit…….moments later this guy comes out with six big boxes of frozen chips on a trolley, loads up the taxi and off we go back to the Blue Dolphin restaurant….arrives back and the queue is now 10 yards long…….I felt I was a Knight in shining armour !!.....lol……knowing all those people waited for their chips to arrive.

 At the taxi rank a women gets in and wants to go to Foreland View, drives off & didn't put the meter on, gets there and I charged her £3.50…..£3.50 she says !!........why is it so expensive….sorry love it's time and a half on Sundays, but I'm only charging you £3.50 and I show her the meter starting price which is £3.90…..she still isn't happy…..starts mumbling about other taxi's don't charge £3.00 maybe you are the only ones……bottom line is, why doesn't she phone them !! ………….Since that day the taxi fares have increased…..God help me if I pick her up again!!!!!!!!

Pulled up outside the Marlborough Club, women gets in and says out loud ' I haven't had you for ages'…….I don't think she realised what she said until I said…..Sorry??……..and we both ended up laughing.

**Sometime people phone up for a taxi and forget to hang up, here are some of the conversations….**

Hello, can I have a taxi please……yes, you can I replied….where and when,  so she gives me her address and says she wants the taxi in 5mins…..ok I replied….then in the back ground I hear a voice when is the taxi coming she says 5mins he says What !!! I told you book it for 10 to 15mins, well I thought you were ready…..well I'm not !!......he's going to be here in a minute so you better hurry up.

Taxi phone rings………Can you pick up a food order from Millennium Chicken??....he says…… what time do you want me to pick it up ? I said………….when can you do it??.... he says……….not until 7.00pm, I said………what time is it now??…….he says….it's 6.25pm….I said……..er…..ok…. and hangs up the phone…..no name….no address…..so he didn't get it.

Picked up an old woman fairly drunk and wants to go to Hostile Park, going up the road and she wants me to stop by the parked cars half way up, she can barely walk (I wonder why), so I helped her out of the taxi, she wants to take a short cut to the back of the houses as to not wake her husband up going through the front door, but the thin s there's a wire fence in the way, now, she ir ts on trying to get over the top of the fence bu ng a fairly big woman there is no way she w o it, she tried a few times with me holding her no …… lres
       So I suggest that I open up m….wf
lower down and she can get betwe

you can imagine what was happening…..couldn't cock her leg over to put between the wires without losing her balance nearly falling over a few times, anyway she does finally get her leg over and starts going through the wire…….this time a light comes on from the house and I am off with her half way through the fence…..well can you imagine what explanation I would have to give !!!!

Picked up a girl from Buddy's worse for wear going to Hillington, all she kept saying was that she is drunk and very sorry, approaching the Wider Road traffic lights and they just turned amber …..stopped and lucky I did, as she open the car door and threw up for the next 5 mins on the road….. saying I'm ready sorry….. I'm ready sorry……..finally got her to Hillington with her still saying…… I'm ready sorry……For once, I was glad to stop at the traffic lights.

Phonings, can we have a taxi in 10mins from the Tunnels going to Score Valley Hotel…..yes I will be there, st wait outside the entrance ……ok they said ….gets down to Tunnels and there's a queue of waiting for taxi's, stopped at the first ones and asked if there are going to Score Valley Hotel, they said no, but asked another couple and they were, so drove over to them, they started to get in and the first couples feller came over thinking it was his taxi, I said no it wasn't, so he went off in a huff cursing & swearing, then his wife came over and asked if I could come back and pick them up……..so where are you going ?…….. she said Langleigh Hotel….ok I said…..I had a booking in about 15mins so I thought that would be ok……………anyway dropped the couple off at Score Valley Hotel and drove back to pick the other couple up……picked them up and off we go to Langleigh Hotel, gets nearly there and the guy says this isn't it…..sorry sir but this is it, no it's at Berry ha ner…..sorry can you repeat that !!......and the wife tries to say it Baer y har or……..do you mean Berrynarbour …..yes… that is it !!!…..and the Hotel is called Langleigh Park Hotel ??........yes, yes that's it……..so off we go 3 miles out of my way and guess what…. I'm already getting late for my next booking.


Arrive to pick up at the Prince of Wales, waits outside for 5mins and this guy comes out walking very slowly and stares at the taxi………a few seconds later he asks if the taxi was for him in a drunken slurred voice.......so looking at him, I said are you going to the High Street ??......yes, he said...........waits for a few seconds and his brain is now engaging.......he finally walks around the taxi and gets in slowly.......so off we go....but guess what he changes his mind and decides to go to the Seahorse half way up the seafront...only has £2.45 so he says he will pay the 5p later and takes a taxi card.......couple hours later he phones up asking for a taxi, pity I was booked for the next half hour, as I would of loved to wait another 10mins outside waiting for him & being short changed again.....not !!!!

Gets a phone call...............hi, my name is Helena.......who's this ???......It's Ricky I said.....do you know me ??......um, no I don't.....well I'm in Barnstaple and I want to get a taxi, now I'm thinking this is a good job coming up.......a pick up from Barnstaple...........well, she says do you know ********...............yes I do know her, well could you get some roll ups from McCoy's and deliver them to her address, but the thing is she hasn't any money, so I will pay for the taxi and the roll ups tomorrow.......sorry love

but the shop has just shut about 2mins ago I said
…..Oh she said, sorry to bother you, thanks
anyway and hangs up.

Biggest Scare when driving a taxi, I was driving
along the road to Mortehoe at about 11.00pm when
in the distance I see a headlight, as it gets closer
the road starts to get narrower, finally this
headlight comes around the corner…….just one
headlight, so me thinking it's a motor bike so we
can both get through…….Oh, no !!!! it's a car with
the inside light not working, how we never hit each
other I will never know.

Picked up a mother and daughter one night, mother
must have been in her 70s and daughter in her 50s,
both totally out of their tree, wanting to go half
way up Avenue Road, now if you know
Ilfracombe, Avenue Road is a very steep road.
Anyway gets there and the mother is sitting in the
front seat of the taxi, so I said to her don't get out
until I come around to help you………did she
listen…….not a hope in hell !!! ……….She gets
out and straight away starts to walk backwards
down the road and as you all know starts getting
quicker and quicker until she trips up and falls

backwards. Thud !!...her head hits the road, her daughter seem to sober up very quickly and as I got to her I said to the daughter I will call a ambulance…..No !! the daughter shouts at me, I can look after her!!!!…..do you want any help….No !!!....you sure I said….. Yes, she says, I can't call a ambulance……..so apart from being yelled at I drove off….went back 5 mins later and no one in sight.

**Sometimes as a taxi driver you say the wrong things to people who has got in the taxi, I normally say hi there!!.......so where do you want to go ??......You can judge by the response if to keep quiet or chat to them…….here are some examples…….**

Picked up a couple + one from a pub in the high street, where are you off to?…. I said, Chandlers Way they said but can you drop my sister off first……so off we go…..pulls outside her house and because her sister had a lot to drink we waited until she opened the door….waited…..and waited…..no good, she couldn't get the key in the lock, passenger got out and let her in……off to

Chandlers Way now, on the way there the woman said they had been married for 44 years…..he said 44 years too long !!...there was a bit of banter between them both for a while, then she asked me how old do you think she was??………

Now this is where it gets complicated as she had a lot of makeup on and I was trying to work out and drive at the same time on how old she was……..well I thought…..44 years married……..married say at around 20 years old……give or take a few years……..that's 64 years….add say 2-3 years……….well about 68 years I said…………..silence for a few seconds then………How old did you say I was!!!!!!!!!….. ( Out loud )…….shouts at her husband….did you hear what the taxi driver said !!!!!!.....shouts at me…….We are nearly at Chandlers Way thank goodness……has another go at her husband…….then we get to Chandlers Way…..he turns to her and says it's her turn to pay…..she is still stunned after what I said…….then there is a few swear words at him and me…she pays….he starts laughing ……she muttering did you hear what the taxi man said about how old I was……He puts his arm around her and says there there………..I don't look 68 do I she says to her husband……..no he said……you look more like 78…..and she storms off up the road.

Guy gets in, Hi mate had a good day???.........I said………no, I f**king haven't he said………..silence for a few moments……….so where do want to go ??.....Queens Av he said………tension like never before complete silence on the way up there….he gets out….gives me the money…..and slams the door…..some mad dude!!!!!

Picked up a rather large women at the rank going to Queens Avenue……….chatting away, gets the Queens Avenue and she pays her money…..she opens the door and she is half way getting out with her rear end facing me and promptly breaks wind in my face…….she says…….oops…..sorry me dear !! …..closes the taxi door and just walks off….

Ok, going back a few years when I started taxi-ing………used to be a guy who would wait opposite the taxi rank in the high street on the other side of the road in a brown coat……now he would appear from nowhere….and wave his hand wanting a taxi he never ever crossed the road…..so, me being number one on the rank I zoom off to pick him up…….what I didn't realise this guy hadn't had a bath for months…..or even years…..he gets in and the smell was horrific…I tried holding my breath……no good…..it was that bad !!!!!…the window was put wide open on my side half way on his side, I was gasping for breath, we were going to Foxbere Road which is about 4-5mins drive……I done it in 2-3mins…..he paid and got out…….I opened every window on the way back to town……feeling quite sick…..I had to get out of the taxi and take some fresh air………….I never picked him up again !!!!….even though he would wave his hand for a taxi…..he actually came around the corner of the rank one day………….never seen 4 taxi's leave the rank so fast!!!!!!!!!!!.

Picked up a guy at Christmas from the Queens and he wants to go to Chambercombe Road, he's totally out of his tree, can hardly speak but I knew where he lived as I have picked him up before, on the way there…… I get a call saying can you pick me up from the High Street in 5 mins I said no problem……… gets to Chambercombe and this guy says he doesn't want to go home now and wants to go back to the High Street, I'm thinking well that's ok, as I have got a pick up there in 5 mins anyway…….gets to the High Street and guess what !!!!!……..he doesn't want to go there, he wants to go to Springfield Road …..now I'm feeling a bit fed up now as I have got someone waiting for a taxi and this guy keeps changing his mind……look mate why don't I drop you off here at the bottom of Springfield Road and you can walk up there……no he would't move and starts getting a bit frisky waving his hands and arms trying to punch me, I stopped and got out….opened his car door and told him to get out the taxi….he's waving his arms still so I grabbed him, got him out and shut the car door……this guy couldn't even stand up, I went and got back in the taxi and he's trying to kick it……and completely misses it by a mile left him spinning around in fresh air as I drove off…..picked this guy up a week later and he didn't remember me or what happened the previous week.

Old guy gets in the taxi, where are you off to mate? He says Hostile Park ok and off we go gets half way there and he says he didn't want to go out but he was bored, I said well it does you good to get out once and awhile, he said well, I don't want to go out but my wife passed away a few months ago and if I stay in I start drinking ( Talking in a loud voice ) Going up Hostile Park when he starts telling me directions to where he lives, wants me to drive up a small parking bay and gets irritated that I reversed up (As it's easier to get out of the cab facing downhill) I tell him the fare is £3 he starts arguing that he only pays £2.50 with another taxi company, I said should of phoned them then, he gives me £3 and walks off muttering to himself.

**Road Rage !!!!!** **Well, I've had my fair share of road rage, some quite funny and some not, here are some that made me and the people I was taking laugh…**..

Picked up 6 people from Lee Bay in our mini bus, coming down into Ilfracombe at Slade Road just enough room for the one lane of traffic as cars were parked all along the main road, get about half way down the line of parked cars when this guy decides to drive up towards me on my side of the road, now me thinking he is going to pull into a space to let me go by.............nope, the dope decides to stop in the middle and drop his wife off and waits for me to reverse, now he only needs to go back say 4-5 yards for me to go by, I need to go back about 50 yards, but no, he stays where he is, so I stopped, turned the bus engine off, hazard lights flashing and gets in the back of the bus to explain what is happening to my 6 passengers, they are all laughing and enjoying what's going on, by this time another car pulls up behind me, then another, then another......so this guy is getting rather annoyed and reverses back 90 mph just missing the parked cars, I started the bus engine, hazards off and as we pass he's giving me the verbal's, I look at him and blew him a kiss.....don't you just love them !!!!!!


Ok... down on Ilfracombe Quay by the Blue Dolphin Restaurant picking up a little old lady who can barely walk and has a Zimmer frame, looks up and down the road all clear to stop outside the restaurant, switched hazards on, (I have to park in the middle of the road as cars are parked all down the road).

Goes in the restaurant to collect the little old lady, takes about 3-4mins comes out and there is a car in front of my taxi and a car behind my taxi..........ok, me thinks that one of these cars will move back so I can get out of the way.....nope !!........gets the lady in the taxi and explains to her that we can't go anywhere at the moment until one of these cars move......5mins went by then the car behind me started to move backwards, so I joined him, had to reverse all the way back to the Sandpiper....about 45 yards ...........all the lady wanted to go to was the Ship & Pilot around the corner.....and not even a thank you from the driver in front of me, just a stare.


**This happened with one fare !!**

10.55pm on a Sunday night and gets a call to pick up from the Grampus Lee Bay going to Woolacombe, ok, I will be there in 10mins. Arrived in about 10 mins and waited outside in the car park put the hazards on so they know I'm there.....waited for about 5 –10 mins so decided to go and see where they are, opens door and shouts "Taxi" and 2 guys put their hands up to acknowledge me, so I went back out to the taxi………waited another 5 – 10mins so off I go back again and shouts " Taxi " !!!!!!

This time they walked out to the taxi, gets in and one wants to be dropped off at Lincombe Cross and the other one wants to go to Croyde **NOT** Woolacombe, so driving off the one that wants to get off at Lincombe Cross says he will walk down to Ilfracombe (about 2 miles) but the other guy said no dude, the taxi driver will take you home, anyway after a lot of…..no I will walk and he will take you home dude we decided to take him as far as The Leas ( Higher Slade ), they exchange phone numbers and off we go to Croyde………well that's where I thought he wanted to go.

Get near the Croyde turning and he decides he wants to go to Woolacombe, on the way you can suss out if the guy is drunk, on drugs etc, etc but this guy, I had no idea what his mind was doing, he told me he was in security, was in the army, Helicopter pilot all sorts of things, but still he had me totally confused!! Arriving in

Woolacombe he wanted a cash machine I pull's outside one and then he asks dude what have I stopped for?? (That is how confusing he was) changing his mind every other minute.

Anyway he gets out and gets some cash, gets back in the taxi and says now what??..........I said you tell me......do you want to go to a pub or Croyde?? yes he says a pub.....where? ..... Well the Jube is over there, so he says ok, I drove over to the car park, he says dude are you coming in for a drink??......sorry mate, I got another job to do (I didn't have, but I just wanted to get away). He says dude how much do you want to stay here while I'm having a drink??........Look mate the meter says £30 that's how much this fare is.....so you are talking another £20 at least if I stay, ok he says and gives me £50 on one condition, that I come in the Jube and have a drink.... Ok..ok, but a small one and we have to leave here at 11.40pm as I have got a job at 12.00 to do (I didn't have one really) goes in the Jube and everyone looks at us, the alarm bells were ringing thinking this guy is going to start a fight......far from it he walks to the bar and buys me a half lager (With a lemonade top) a pint for himself, starts chatting to a young lad and buys him a drink, then he buys another pint and a double JD and coke and another half for me , plus I wanted some peanuts so he brought them (Well he was buying).

The young lad rolled him a cigarette and he lit it in the pub, I told him he can't do that, so did the young lad so he walked outside to light it. By this time he has one sip of his pint so I told him he's got 10mins then I'm off !!.......puts the second half of lager he brought me behind the bar while he wasn't looking, ate the peanuts and went outside to see what he was up to.....still his first pint was only a quarter down ,so I said, time to go, either you want me to take you to Croyde or you walk there.....the young lad said this place closes in 15 minutes so he decides he wanted to go, and gives the drinks he brought to this young lad.

Off we go to Croyde up Potters Hill, he starts telling me I'm going the wrong way but then shuts up when he finds out I'm not, gets to The Thatched Inn Croyde and he says again dude coming in for a drink ??.....sorry mate, I got 6mins to get back to Ilfracombe and with that he gets out and shakes my hand and says thanks for my help, he crosses the road and .....I AM OFF LIKE A BAT OUT OF HELL!!!!!!!!. Hope I never meet him again he was some weird dude!!!!!

Sitting on the rank waiting for a fare when the taxi car door opens and a guy pokes his head in and says how much to John Fowlers Holiday Park.......I said about £4.00, his wife standing behind him (with a face on) says why is it so expensive ?? we were told by another taxi driver it would be £3.50, So I said ok, I will do it for that but I will put the meter on to show them the true cost, meter started at £3.90.

On the way up the wife sitting in the back seat with her 2 kids starts moaning about the cost of taxi's and why it was dearer on a Sunday, so I had to explain to her that if she worked on a Sunday would she work for normal time ??.....Her son in the meantime keeps on saying to her stop moaning about the fare, anyway gets to John Fowlers Holiday Park and the fare says £4.28......the women still moaning and the son telling her again to stop and the guy pays the fare.

Picked up a food order from Millennium Chicken going to Twitchen Park Woolacombe, puts the meter on and on arrival met the person who ordered the takeaway, meter read £21.40 food order came to £26.10 thinking that there is no way he will pay the fare so I charged him £12, He gets a bit annoyed saying why does it cost that much as he was quoted £5 for delivery.

I told him there is no way it is £5 delivery even on a weekday, so I phoned up Millennium Chicken and put it on loud speaker for him to listen, the girl without any prompt from me said that she didn't quote any delivery price as she didn't know how much it would be. He then back tracked saying he didn't order it his wife did, so as the car phone was ringing for jobs to do I told him that I would take it back if he didn't pay more than the £5 for delivery in the end we settle for £9 which although it was well below the price I wanted, at least I got rid of the food which was getting cold.

Picked up a guy with a bottle in his hand, ask me to take him to Torrs Park, as we are driving he tells me that he hasn't been home for 2 days and reckons his other half has changed the locks, going along the high street he sees a mate and starts waving the bottle and shouts at him, we turn down towards Torrs Park and all of a sudden there's this big bang and we both duck thinking something has hit the car or we were shot at……….what it was that by waving the bottle the top blew off and the cork hit the roof of the taxi and flew around the cab just missing us.

Just going to start my shift when the boss (Colin) phones me up and says he will pick me up outside my house in the taxi I would be driving that night, 5 mins later he arrives and we swap seats, he's off out and I dropped him off at the Prince of Wales, on the way there he tells me that I have the Taxi phone and Diary. I then dropped him off with his wife Marlyn at the Prince of Wales.

I then went off to do a taxi job, after about 20mins, I started to wonder if the phone was working has it hadn't rung, looked around in the cab and no phone, got the other driver to call it......not ringing, looked again and I can't find it anywhere. Tried phoning the boss......no answer, Decided to go down to the Prince of Wales before the boss left there, on arrival he saw me pull up, I got out and went inside to see if he had the taxi phone, he said no it's in the cab, we both went outside and he continued to say it's in the cab and started to look for it saying it's in here somewhere...............after about 2-3 mins looking, with a look that could kill his wife came out with the taxi phone in her hand............it was in his jacket pocket all along !!!!!!! with 8 missed calls.

Later that night I get a call and someone wants a price for a taxi to Combe Martin, so I said where about's in Combe Martin do you want to go?? She said the High street, so I said where about's in the High street considering it's the longest in the UK (over 2 miles long) she replied I am going to the High street, so I quoted her a price from the start and half way up the high street………she then said she would phone me later……she never did.

Another night and half way through my shift when a guy phones me up and says he wants a food order picked up from MacDonald's Barnstaple, could I come and meet him to give me the food order, so off I go and meet him thinking it's a small order here is what he wanted ;

4 x Big Mac meals with 3 x Strawberry, 1 Banana drinks.

2 x Chicken Burger.

1 x Kids meal with Nuggets.

2 x Box of Chicken Nuggets.

11 x Plain Double Cheese Burgers.

1 x Fillet Ofish (What ever that is).

1 x Big Mac.

Plus 4 Coke drinks and Straws, Ketchup & Napkins.

He gives me money for the food and tells me to take the taxi fare out of it as well.

Arrives at MacDonald's and goes to the drive through and starts giving him the order, when I get to the 11 Plain Double Cheese Burgers the guy taking the order said that he needs to get the manager, speaks to the manager and he confirms the order and said it will be about 15 – 20 mins, drives around to pay and pick up the order by this time there was a long queue behind me. Started to load on the food and drinks and 10mins later off I go back to Ilfracombe .

Next job a food order from Millennium Chicken going to Cook Island, picks up the food and half way up Mullacott Millennium Chicken phones and said that they have given me the wrong order, turns around and heads back to Millennium Chicken, picks up the right order and goes to Cook Island, coming back down from Mullacott Millennium Chicken phones again and said that they forgot to give me a bottle of Coke with the delivery, so back I go to Millennium Chicken to pick up the Coke and go back up to Cook Island………in the mean time someone phones up and asked if I could pick up her Laptop she left behind when I picked her up earlier, didn't know when I could do it as I was thinking maybe there is something else Millennium Chicken had forgotten to give me !!!!!

One night half way through my shift when a girl phones me up and says she wants a taxi from tunnels going to Woolacombe House Hotel, I arrive and this girl is crouching down near a wall by the entrance she sees me and gets up and opens the car door and says just wait a minute driver and shuts the door again…..I'm now hearing that she is having a big argument with her boyfriend by the taxi. She opens the door again and gets in sits down then gets out of the taxi again to confront her boyfriend again !!……….seconds later she gets in cursing her boyfriend because he wouldn't give her the room key and says she wants to go to Woolacombe House Hotel, I drive off, now not sure where this place is so decided to ask her roughly where it is.........after a few questions & answers it was Widerscombe House Hotel where she wanted to go.

On the way, we started to talk and I find that her boyfriend has had too much to drink and she wanted to go back to the hotel get her bankers card (as she didn't have any money) to pay for the taxi and leave him and hers friends at the wedding party, I persuaded her to go back to the party and try and sit with her friends and ignore her boyfriend...which she did on the condition that I would pick her up Asap if it didn't work out. So dropped her off after getting her money..............2 hours later she phones and want a taxi ASAP !!!! I go and pick her up........alone, no boyfriend in site and she tells me it didn't work so I took her back to Widerscombe House Hotel, she still didn't have the front door key and had to phone the hotel to let her in, and thanked me for helping her.


Same night, woman phones up and asked for a return taxi from St Brannocks Park Road to Jack's

Dairy ,….yep no problem I said, she then asked how much it would be ??, as she had one on Friday and it cost her £5.00 and her friend told her that was too much, so I said what time on Friday as it is time and a half after 11.30pm, she said it was before, so I said it would be £4.00 return……….she was happy with that and waited for me.

Picked her and her dog up which I told her to keep in the foot wells as I didn't want the dogs hair everywhere, she got in a strop saying that her dog was a pedigree and it never loses its hair and goes to shows etc etc, etc, she then said do all the taxis have a data base and different numbers which I said yes we have different numbers, why I asked (And I know I shouldn't have said that) Oh just wondered why different taxis turn up that's all.

About 10.40pm I get a phone call from Horne Park garages asking if I could take 3 Canadian people to The School House Kentisbury their car had broken down and was towed to the Mullacott garage, he said he had already phoned some other taxi up and they quoted £25 - £30 but couldn't get there until 11.30, so I said yes that's about the right price, So

I arrived there, loaded there suite cases in the taxi and off we go.

He had a tablet which showed him the directions but coming from Porlock in Somerset, so I said as I didn't know where this school house was could he give me the post code so I could get it up on my mobile, he said there wasn't one, as we were going along he asked how much it would be? I told him it would be around £25 - £30 he started to panic so I said no more than £30.

Thinking he had a map coming from Porlock I went to Easter Close Cross which is the turning down to Kentisbury, just as I get there the taxi phone rings a guy asked for a taxi from Weatherspoon's to John Fowlers thinking am almost there ,I said about 30 mins which he was happy with. Gets to Easter Close Cross and about to turn down to Kentisbury when to guy said no no no it's not this place!!!!!…. So I said let me have a look at your tablet and the address was Countisbury, Lynmouth Somerset **with** a post code.

I said to them that we are nowhere near this address it's miles away, but as I had them in the taxi I had to get them there. So off we go to Lynmouth, gets to the garage where you go to

Lynmouth and the guy says the sign post read A39 Porlock (which is on his tablet) so carrying on up the road for a mile when we come across a pub, I decided to go in and ask for directions, mean time the meter is reading £65. Found out where to go, had to go back and drive through Lynmouth up Countisbury Hill pass the Blue Boar Inn over a cattle grid and should be just down the road………
So done that driving along looking for the School House when the phone rings the guy asking where the taxi they ordered 30 mins ago was, I apologised and apologised told him there was nothing I could do as I was at the top of Lynmouth in Somerset he hung up, 2 mins later his girlfriend decided to give me grief for about 5 mins then hung up. Carried on driving for about 5 mins and came across a signpost saying Lynmouth 5 miles which meant we missed the signpost saying School House, the woman got a signal and arranged there friends to come to the main road with torches, so I turned around and about 3 mins later we see all these torches on the road so I pulled over and hugs and handshakes all round, the woman crying with relief, the old guy in the front seat really stressed out, so I only charged them £85……what a journey!!!!!

Pulls up outside the Bunch of Grapes, waits for a few minutes next thing 2 people come out one holding the other………They open the front passenger door and the other women helps the other one to get in, me thinking I got one here !!!.......off we go to Montpelier Terrace, gets there and after a while she finds the taxi fare money and decides to get out the taxi, as you all know there is a field with sheep opposite the terrace, next thing she stumbles back against the barb wire fence and gets stuck and can't move, saying I'm stuck in a slurred voice and tries moving but no she's getting more hooked up by the minute, so I get out the cab and pulls her off the fence with a large ripping sound and help her around the taxi to the steps, I point her in the right direction and off I drive.


Picked a gentleman up from the pier at 5.45pm to take him to Bideford, on the way there over the radio there is a warning that the bridge is closed and queues of traffic going in and out of Barnstaple, so I go the Muddiford route gets to the hospital and the queue started there, in the meantime 2 ambulances and a police car with blue lights going comes up the road, makes our way to the traffic lights and still listening to the radio bulletin's decided to go through the town and get on the link road at the top of Newport.

Still loads of traffic everywhere but eventually gets on the link road , gets to Bideford at 7.00pm and the gentleman asks if I could take him home which thinking about it with the traffic as it is should be ok, by this time I was starting to want to go the loo, drops him off and needing the loo asap, drives down to the quay where the toilets are and parks up and rushes over to the toilets…….only to find they are locked !!!!!! Thinking where else is there a toilet….Morrison's !! so I quickly go over there parks up and leaves my money bag in the car, done the business and goes back to Ilfracombe, gets back about 7.50pm, goes home only to find I left my money bag in the car so had to go back and get it (Senior moment) so finished at 8.10pm.

Had a phone call on the way to dropping off a customer,  she says can you pick up a bag of Sugar and 2 Milky Bars they are on offer at the counter at the Premier shop in the high street 50p each, yep I can do that I said, took her address and it's on my way to dropping off other customers (Stuart, the bosses son and wife Clair), Stuart said he would get it for me to save me from getting out of the cab, He comes back no Milky Bars on offer so brought them for £0.65 = Total =£2.80. Arrives at the address and knocks on the door......no answer.....knocks again and a women opens it, I explained that there was no Milky Bars on offer only at £0.65 each, she didn't say much gave me a load of cash and a £5 note and quickly shut the door.

Back in the cab I checked what she gave me total =£10 so that was a easy fare !!!!!


Picked up off the rank and they want to go to Higher Slade farm, half way there and they start to have a barney, she said to him..... did you really have to give that girl a cuddle you know I have a issue with her, he said she needed comforting...... she said yes, but six times!!!!! He starts laughing which makes her even more angry, I suppose I have to pay for the taxi as well, yep, I haven't any money on me he said, she pays muttering away and storms off to her house, he gets out and I wished him luck.

Just dropped of a customer at Braunton when I get a phone call from Tim saying could I go to Red Barn Woolacombe on the way back to pick up a guy who wants to go to Ilfracombe, yep, no problem on my way. Arrives at the Red Barn Woolacombe at about 2.20am and no one there, looks around and decides to drive around the other side to see if he was waiting at the side of the Red Barn, get half way round and there is a guy standing in the middle of the road with his hand held up……stops in front of him and lowers the passenger side window.

Are you going to Ilfracombe ???? I said, No, he said we want to go to Croyde and as he said that, another guy gets in the back of the cab, sorry mate I'm booked to go to Ilfracombe I said to him, I sensed this guy wasn't going to move, so I phoned my controller Tim to check what to do and he said it was ok to take them as the person I was supposed to pick up was not here. So the other guy gets in the back and said he is staying at a B&B no name or street just a post code **EX33 1LZ**, so off we go to Croyde on the way he mentions the Thatched Inn, yep I know where that is (Meanwhile the other guy falls asleep), Gets to the

Thatched Croyde stops and the guy said no this isn't it, so, I said what is the post code ?? He says **EX33 1LZ** ok, we are here no he said it's further up the road, ok so off we go through Croyde and on to the Saunton road, he's still checking his phone and giving me directions.

It's 7 mins away pass Saunton Sands Hotel I said to him do you remember this hotel, no he said, I was looking at the sat-nav when we came here this morning, he said is there any place to eat around here?? At this time of night 3.00am on the Saunton road.. no, I said, gets to crossroads and he tells me to turn left up a country lane to a place called LOBB gets 20 yards up the road and he now tells me we are going in the wrong direction, had to reverse back down as there was no turning point, gets back on the Saunton road again and he said the B&B is in Braunton, drives to Braunton and parks at a bus stop on the main road, look mate I don't want to drive around and take your money, and the meter is still running so he decides to get out of the taxi and tries to wake up his mate, mate wakes up and refuses to leave the taxi saying there is no way he was getting out as they didn't know where they were, so I said to him, does he know where the B&B is …???

So he looks on his phone and guess what !!!!!!!
the post code is **EX33 1LJ** so I put it on my phone
and finds that we went pass it on the Saunton road,
they both start moaning about how much this is
costing them, so off we go back up the Saunton
road gets to the point on my phone and I stop
again, right this is where the post code is, guy said
you need to turn around so I turn around again
goes down the road comes to a small junction he
says turn right…..turns right and he yells that's my
motor…….I think to myself  AT
LAST !!!!!!......time 3.30am decide to give them a
bit off the fare as the guy behind me was getting a
bit irate, and I was glad to be heading home !!!!!!!


Sitting on the taxi rank when a couple comes
around the corner looking like they have had a few
to many, guy sits in the front and the woman sits in
the back, I drove off and the woman tries to start
talking ,but she is so intoxicated I don't understand
her, gets to Foreland View and stops outside their
house, this is where the fun starts……That will be
£3 please I said, He starts looking in his pockets
decides to get out of the taxi to check his pockets
even more swaying back and forwards he said I've

no money dear can you pay him ?? She now starts looking into her hand bag and finds her purse, opens her purse and money flies everywhere as she had her car door open, so the guy starts looking on the ground and finds the money she dropped (I think).

She hands me 2 coins and said here's £2 , I said sorry love it's £1.20 you have just given me, she looks again and starts to give me 2x10p, 2x5p & 3x 1p is that enough she says, sorry love there is only £1.53p and the fare is £3.00. I said haven't you got any money in the house ?? he then says…..hold on!!, I got some and you can have it as a tip, walks to the house which is about 5 yards away, I'm looking at him and he can't find the key hole to put the key in, after about 5 mins with the woman still looking through her hand bag he finally opens the door and disappears…….minutes later he opens the taxi door and arrives with a tin full of 1p & 2p coins see photo……the women that I can't except all this, so she said take 3 bags of coins and that should pay for the taxi, so I took 2 bags she decides to get out of the taxi opens the front door nearly falling in, I hand her the tin full of money and she slowly turns around swaying back and forwards walking towards the house, I couldn't watch as if she trips the money would fly

everywhere, so I quickly turned the taxi around and went off to my next job.

**I've had my fair few of things going wrong with a taxi car, here are some true stories……..**Been working a shift when about 9.00pm decided to have a break, pulls outside my house and forgets to take the ignition key out, goes inside has a coffee then goes to get in the car and it has locked its self, can't get in and the phone going ten to a dozen, phones the boss and he didn't have the spare key but another driver did, so after about 20mins the boss turns up with the spare key, I got let back into my taxi, never left the keys in the car after that !!!!!

Had a job picking up in Braunton on a very cold and windy night in winter, gets pass Mullacott and after about a mile I heard this strange noise…………it sounded like a flat tyre…..it was a flat tyre!!!!…….pulled over in a lay-by and with the wind howling and pitched dark had a go changing the wheel. Phoned in to say what had happened, so they sent another taxi to Braunton………..15mins later the other driver pulled up next to my taxi, smiled and said…….it's a bit nippy tonight……and drove off…..leaving me trying to change a tyre in the dark and freezing cold.

Gets in the taxi to start my shift, notice the fuel gauge at just over a quarter full, half way into the night and after 3 jobs out of Ilfracombe I notice the yellow fuel warning light on and with another 2 out of town jobs booked for later, I decided to swap taxi's, goes out to change taxi's and get all my stuff into the other taxi turned the ignition on.......and guess what!!!!.....that has less fuel in it than the one I just got out of........so, off I go to the other taxi and that has just about enough fuel for the night.


Get a phone call from a young lady wanting a taxi at the top of Horne Road, arrives and standing on the corner were 2 people, after winding down the window I asked them if it was them who ordered the taxi, girl replies yes, it's us and do you like banana's ?? (I thought to myself the night was a bit quiet) she gets in with her dad, she starts waving a banana in my face saying this ones quite cute do you fancy that one ??? as we have 18 to take home and my mum doesn't like banana's. (Didn't like to ask where they got the 18 banana's).

I said that one will do fine, her dad tells her to stop waving the banana around while I'm driving, so on the way there she says do I pick up many funny people in my taxi ?? so I told her one of my stories she laughs and when we get to the address she hands me another banana, her dad pays the fare and I end up with 2 banana's as a tip.

Picks up a couple from the Queens to go to Marlborough Way as they get in a young girl asks them if they had money to pay for the taxi fare they both replied Yes, the girl gives them her front door key and tells them to look after it and she will see them later after they finish their pool match, so off we go to Marlborough Way, arrives and he didn't have any money and asks his partner (who was a bit drunk) if she had any and starts looking in her purse…………..nothing!! Do you mind taking me to a cash point he says I will give you £6 for you troubles, so off to the High street we go, he hands me the girls front door key, why ?? I don't know as the girl sitting next to him wasn't going nowhere, gets back in and off we go to Marlborough Way again !! he pays and both get out of the taxi and walk towards the house.

Sitting on the taxi rank 1 hour later and guess what!!!! It's the girl from the Queens, she gets in with 2 other guys and on the way to Marlborough Way she asks me if I was the taxi driver who took her friend's home….I replied yep…. eventually (Should have said no) they had no money, so I had to take them to a cash point, on the way to Marlborough Way this girl swears every other words and kept on asking me if I saw the couple I took up there earlier go in the house, I replied if I waited for every person to go in there house I wouldn't do many fares!! She says she has only one key and did I see them go in the house again!!!! We eventually get there and she storms out of the taxi and runs to her house, leaving the other 2 guys to pay, one guy says that was his sister I said good luck with that one tonight.


Got a phone call from Sandy Cove Hotel, young lady on the phone wants a taxi to take her to a shop, asks which is the nearest I said probably C/ Martin but I'm not sure if any are open now, as it was gone 10.30pm, she said could I come and pick her up and take her to Combe Martin ASAP, I said no problem I am on my way.

Gets there and 2 girls are waiting outside the hotel, they get in and this girl had a lovely broad Yorkshire accent she says can we go to the nearest shop to buy some cigarettes and I said I think the shop on the seafront is still open so off we go, on the way there she tells me that since she has arrived for her friend's wedding people have been unkind with her accent as most people can't understand her, I assured her I can understand her and think the accent was quite cute.

Finds the shop and the 2 girls get out only to find it had closed 2 mins before, one of the girls bangs on the door to attract the sales woman but she said she can't open the shop they get back in the taxi a little distraught, I said I think there is another shop open further up the high street (which brighten up they faces) so off we go again, gets to the next shop and it's open, they both go inside again and I can see they are chatting away to the shopkeeper for about 5mins.

They eventually come out and gets back in the taxi with cigarettes and a bottle of drink, head back to Sandy Cove Hotel, on the way she says that I have been the nicest man she has met here (Which means I am doing my job well) half way there and the taxi phones rings..........hello

'A' taxi's I said, this guy on the other end starts talking in a mad voice about something, I said sorry sir but where do you want the taxi from ?? He still didn't tell me and then eventually hangs up, I said to the girls I get some phone calls like that, phone rings again ..........hello 'A' taxi's I said...............guess what same guy, ranting about something and me trying to find where he wants his taxi from, next minute the girl behind me says that's my boyfriend talking, so she starts talking to him and he's ranting and raving where are you? Where did you go? I thought you were going to leave a cigarette for me and she is trying to explain that we are about 2 mins away but he has gone off on one!!!! I didn't like the way he was talking to her so I hung up.

Pulls in to Sandy Cove Hotel and within seconds her boyfriend appears pulls open the rear taxi door starts ranting and snatches the cigarettes from her hand and slams the door, I said to her is that your boyfriend ? she says unfortunately yes, in a sad voice, well he looks like he's on one I said, anyway we start to sort out the taxi fare and a few minutes pass when all of a sudden the taxi door flies open again and guess what !!!!! it's the boyfriend again !!! Sticks his head in the taxi looking all around like a chicken looking for food says what's going on here?

 She's says she is paying for the taxi and he starts ranting and raving, I said to him did he want another taxi ?? ( Which didn't help) and he pulls her out of the taxi, her friend said thanks for a great time and being very helpful he's just a little drunk......I through to myself that poor girl could do better.


**So this section is number 3 in the series, here are some more true taxi stories, and with a little help from my fellow taxi driver and friend Tim James whose been a taxi driver for over 25 years, I'm sure you will find this very funny.......**

As a taxi driver you have to be a few things i.e **Patience, Calm, Honest, Having a Sense of Humour & Be Understanding......**
**Patience** - because sometime they don't have money to pay the fare or they can't find it.

**Calm** - is when they give you the wrong address, they still can't find the fare money and you are getting late for the next fare.

**Honest** - is when they give you £20 note thinking it's a £5 note and say keep the change, or you tell them what they don't want to hear.

**Having a Sense of Humour -** Is when they say something and you give them a reply they want to hear.

**Being Understanding** - is when they have problems with their girlfriend/boyfriend and you act as an agony aunt trying to solve their problems, this is where **Honest** kicks in and after giving them good advise **Having a Sense of Humour** sometimes finds **Calm** kicking in for being **Patience !!!!**….

**Sometimes personal things are left behind in the taxi i.e  Bankers Card, Driving Licence, Lipstick, Jackets, Mobile Phones and a Dog…..Yes a Dog !!!!!.**

1.

I used to pick up a guy called Andy and his lovely Alsatian dog, now you are thinking how on earth can you carry a big Alsatian dog !!!, well he used to call a taxi and we would pull up, he would open the boot the dog would happily jump in, he would close the boot get in and tell me where he would want to go and as always, not very far.......walking distant, one time we were talking so much he paid the fare got out the taxi and walked off went about 10 yards down the road and before I could pull away he came running back to get the dog, I even forgot it was there....lol.

2.

Picked up a couple from the seafront at about 10.30pm going to John Fowlers Holiday Park, dropped them off and went to do another job, after about 10 minutes under my drivers seat, came a light and a vibration this lasted for about 10 seconds, I knew exactly what that was ......... a Mobile phone.

So I carried on doing the next fare as I knew it was under my drivers seat and going nowhere, off it went again about 10 seconds but no light this time just the vibration this went on for about 10 minutes, thinking I should retrieve it ASAP as the mobile phone battery will go flat, so I pulled over after finishing my last fare ….but no mobile phone, looked everywhere even with my taxi torch….nothing !!!

Just about to get back in the taxi to do another fare when the mobile phone went off again !!!! I quickly got out looked under my drivers seat and found the mobile phone had vibrated under the cars carpet into a small hole (Like the Black Hole of Calcutta), luckily, I had my torch or I would never of found it !!!. Answered the phone and the man on the other end was in a lot of stress (Well you know and I know if you can't find your mobile it's like the end of the world) he was so relieved I answered it and I took it back to him asap, when I got there, there was a nice tip waiting for me.

**3.**
I decided to go to Crete for my 50<sup>th</sup> birthday (seems like yesterday) and unknown to me and my partner, two of the people I have picked up in my taxi in Ilfracombe took the same flight, After landing at Heraklion airport, I proceeded to the baggage conveyor and my partner who knew the same people spotted them waiting for their baggage to come around on the conveyor, I double

checked this and quickly got behind them and to their astonishment  they turned around and I said…….'A' Taxi's welcome's you to Crete and your taxi is waiting outside……what a jaw dropping moment !!!

And the funny thing is we both caught the same transfer bus and they stayed 50 yards down the road from us, we went out a few times for a meal or to after that, what a great holiday!!!!!!

4.

Had a job to pick up 3 girls from Tiverton Parkway going to the Health Farm at Torrs, I only had the 4 seater taxi as I didn't expect there would be much luggage……silly me!!!........waited by the station exit and these 3 girls must have had luggage for 6 to 8 people, so I got the girls in the taxi and started to load the taxi with all this luggage…. boot full (and it was a big boot in that car), in the end I had to put 1 case and 3 holdalls on the back seat strap them in, It was a bit of a squash but got it all in and could see why they needed to go to a Health Farm…….lol.

5.

Picked up a food order of 2 pizza's going to Slade, arrived at the place and to my astonishment the lady said she didn't want it anymore and refuse to pay for it and shut the door on me, thinking what do I do now!!!!!… so I took the pizzas back, told them what happened and ask for my money back….. plus the fare, the guy at Chicken land gave me my fare and money back and said I might as well have the pizza's as they are no good to him, so I went back to the taxi rank and share the pizza's with my fellow taxi drivers…….. Mmmm.

6.

Picked up two guys, one worse for wear gets to the first address and the guy asks how much is the taxi fare? I replied £4.20 so he puts his hand in his pocket and hands me loads of change and says is that enough??, I counted it out and it came to £1.79, sorry sir that's not enough, hold on he says laughing to himself here's some more money and hands it to me…….sorry sir that's now £1.83….still laughing to himself and the other guy saying don't worry I'll pay it, he then says give me back the money I gave you, I've found some more in my pocket……and he's still laughing gets some more money out of his pocket……..yes £2.40 so we hunt for the £1.83 I gave back to him and after 5 minutes we get to £4.20, he gets out and guess what!!!!…he's still laughing.

7.

Taxi phone rings…….Hello, can I have a taxi please ?…..yes, I said where from and where to ??…..I don't know where I am !! she said, ok, can you describe to me anything around you…. well, I'm in a Gallery…..good.. I said, where ?? ….down the seafront….ok there are many galleries down Ilfracombe seafront, what's outside ??…….there is a big green mound…….I'm looking at it now she says….this green mound has it got grass on it…..yes….yes it has !!, well, that's called Capstone Hill, I know where you are just stay there, I will be there in 5 minutes.

8.

One Boxing Day night the phone rings and a woman wants me to buy her a quarter bottle of Vodka, I said any particular make ?? …….no, she replied as it was quiet, I thought I might as well do it, so off I go to the off licence, Got the quarter bottle of Vodka for £4.49 plus the taxi fare which was £4.20 that came to £8.69.

Arrived at the destination rang the door bell a woman opened the door, I gave her the bottle of Vodka and she gave me £25.00, before I could say anything she said keep the change and shut the door, so that's what I did I kept it!!.

Phone rings again 2 hours later and guess what !!!!!… it's that lady wanting another quarter bottle of Vodka, so I through to myself that I would get her another one but not charge her for it as she gave me too much last time, arrives at the house knocks and rings the doorbell …….no one comes to the door….. knocks again and rings the doorbell again……nothing !!……thinking now what am I going to do with this bottle of Vodka ??……..knocks again and I can hear someone shouting …..come in !!…..come in !!.

Thinking this could be one of these moments, a deep breath and I slowly turned the door handle and slowly opened the front door and slowly walked in, this is where your mine kicks in……….is she behind the door with a empty bottle of Vodka ready to hit me over the head and me waking up like in the movie Misery (1990) !!!!!, In the movie, this woman kidnaps a famous author……hold on a minute I'm an author !!!……now it's time to stop thinking like that !!!!!……or maybe she is in her birthday suit….stop it and focus, I'm saying to myself !!!!!……focus Ricky please focus !!!!!!!.

I'm thinking now with the lady still saying…. come in !!….. come in !!, I got to the hallway and it's dimly lit and daylight coming through the hallway window and there she is !!!!, ….standing in her living room doorway with a £20 note in her hand fully clothed (Thank Goodness), and again…. before I can say anything to her she takes the bottle of Vodka and tells me to keep the change, I didn't want to upset her and did try to explain that £20 is far to much, but she would have none of it !!!!, so thinking where I was, And the movie Misery, I quickly got out of the house and hoped she didn't phone me again that night!!!!!!!……..…she didn't.

9.
Picked up a foreign lady from the health farm at Torrs Park, she wants to go to the cinema, not Ilfracombe cinema but the Barnstaple cinema…..no problem and off we go, do you know how much this will be she asks ???……well, it's

going to be £25 each way as I can't wait for you and I need to come back to Ilfracombe…..ok, she says……we get to Barnstaple outside the cinema and she hands me a £50 note.

She asked if they would except a £50 note at the cinema ??, I don't know I replied, I tell you what, I will go in and ask them, gets out of the taxi goes into the cinema and asked if they would except a £50 note as the lady in my taxi has no change……looking a bit confused the girl behind the counter asks her manager and he said yes, it would be ok, so I checked when the film ended told the lady what time I would pick her up…… sorted !!

10.
In the last year we have had taxi cams fitted, not for violence against our drivers but to save guard against it, here is one instance where it became useful…….

Gone 11.30pm picked up a girl in Ilfracombe who wanted to go to Barnstaple, arrives at the destination and the meter read £28, so I said to her that will be £28 please, she replied I only got £3.50…….This is where taxi-ing gets so annoying !!!!……so why did you have a taxi when you know you can't pay for it I said to her…….I don't know she replied....well, you do know you are being recorded on the taxi cam, this made her think, well.... she said.. hear is my mobile phone number and my address, I can pay tomorrow, I phoned her mobile just to check it was the right one and it was, the next day my boss phoned her and got the rest of the money.

11.
Sometimes we are late picking up a fare, here is an example why this happens !!.......Went to pick up 5 guys wanting to go to Ilfracombe high street, arrived outside the house parked on their driveway, 5 guys came out of the house with open bottles of beer in there hands.

  Well, there is one thing I don't allow is alcohol in the taxi cab, open or in a glass so this is where it gets interesting........Sorry guys, no beer in the taxi...... I said...... some drink it straight away and get in the taxi, some moan and get in the taxi and there is always one who argues that he won't spill it even through he can hardly stand up !!!

    Sorry mate, you either drink it now or put it over there on the floor out of harms way or stay here......Still he's arguing and still I'm sticking to my guns !!.......So after 5 - 6 minutes the other guys that are all waiting in the taxi tell him to drink it and get in the taxi, he ends up leaving it on the floor and where this pick up should of taken 3 minutes at the most it took 10 minute……now you can understand why we are sometimes late !!!!

By the Way, if you soil the taxi seats it's a £75 fee.

12.
Working with a fellow taxi driver named #### and over the radio comes his voice…..Ricky, I need some help fast !!!!, where are you ???….. I replied….I'm up Torrs he said sounding in a desperate voice, can you hurry !!!!… ok, I'll be there in a minute and I race up there.

   Up Torrs there are a lot of hotels which branch off down from the main road leaving a small step (not big enough for railings) but big enough to watch out for, …….well, arriving half way up Torrs I come across #### ….he's in a right panic !!!. What he had done was that while he was turning the 6 seater taxi around he accidentally dropped the 2 back wheels over one of these small steps outside one of these hotels……We both looked at each other and said how are we going to get these back wheels over the step ????, as they were suspended off the ground and the taxi was resting on it's belly.

First we tried lifting the back up with the handbrake off…..nothing doing…….so we flagged down another taxi driver and we started lifting the back while  ####  drove the taxi forward, with a little bit of luck the 2 back tyres gripped and the taxi shot forward…….until now this has been our little secret and as he is still driving a taxi, I will not mention his name…….. or will I !!!!!!!!!

13.

A new takeaway had just opened  and we had the contract to deliver the food, I think I must have broken a few records that one night when I did over 15 takeaways, that was not so bad but every time I had to collect them, I had to park down the road and go up a flight of stairs to pick them up, at one stage a person had phoned up complaining during the evening that the takeaway was cold, I was not surprised as at one point, I had 3 orders to deliver at 3 different locations in Ilfracombe….boy, was I knackered after doing that shift !!!!!!!

14.

As I was dropping off a customer, I notice a lady sitting on the steps of the taxi office on Marlborough  Road , I reversed back and asked if she was waiting for a taxi as the office was closed all day being bank holiday, Yes, she said I've been waiting for 25 minutes…. ok, do you want me to take you home ???…..Yes, and she got in the taxi…..as we were pulling away she started to say that everyone has gone from the high street and tried to tell me that I was going the wrong way, I didn't pay much attention to that but she started to say some weird sentences, and not thinking to hard I through this woman has some sort of Dementia which she later admitted, anyway I get her home and only charged normal fare……sorry boss…..didn't have the heart to charge her full fare as she had been waiting 25 minutes for a taxi and was very confused.

15.
Picked up a fare from the High Street Ilfracombe going to Hostile Park, last time I picked him up he was in a bad mood, so I through I would tread very carefully this time, we get to Hostile Park and like last time he wants me to drive up a small driveway to his front door to get him as near as possible,  but

this driveway is on a quite a big slop which would be hard for him to get out of the taxi facing upwards and it's easier getting out facing downwards, so I reversed up to where I could go no further, he's mumbling that he has to walk further but I said to him I would help him up the slope.

I got him out of the taxi and he is really unsteady on his feet (Maybe it's all the alcohol he has consumed) so, off we go heading towards his front door, we're nearly there when there is a big gust of wind which knocks us both sideways, I hold on to him like my life depended on it and we both get thrown towards a pickup truck……and guess who was in the middle between the truck and the guy……me !!! …….ouch that hurt !!!!

I finally get him upright again and get to his front door……he says he normally uses another taxi firm……(wish he had)…..anyway got a 50p tip out of it !!!!…..lol.


16.
Gone 2.00am and picked a girl off the rank going to Higher Slade, just pulled away when she decides to put her feet on the dash board…..Sorry

luv can you please take your feet off the dash board and sit up properly…..with a huff she does what she's told, by the time I get to the end of the high street she is fast asleep……..gets to higher Slade and pulls over, radios in to my other taxi driver what has happen and tries to wake this girl up, she stirs and gives me £5 for the fare (which isn't enough, but was glad to get some sort of payment)….she then goes back to sleep….wakes her again…….and she starts to get out of at the taxi and looks like she is sleep walking……where do you live luv ??……..and she points to a dark lane…..well, there is no way I am taking her down there, as she could accuse me of anything as she was so drunk, so I pointed her in the right direction and she walks slowly down the lane…..waited a few minutes just in case she falls over or shouts for help hears the gate and front door opening then nothing, so drove off…..these are some predicaments that taxi drivers have to be so careful with and I through I handled that really well.

17.

Working one Saturday night and picked up a girl who I have known for years...... Tina, took her to the Liberal Club and on the way there she asked if I could pick her up later about 10.30pm so I booked it in with our controller Gaynor and said I will see you later, well from 10.00pm onwards we were very busy running around trying to keep everyone happy and Gaynor told me at about 10.20pm to pick up Tina at 10.30pm well, I completely forgot, Tina phones up at 10.40pm asking where her taxi was, Gaynor tells her I been and done it, Gaynor radio's to me did you do the 10.30pm at the Liberal Club ????? I said no, but I'm on my way.......arrives outside the Liberal Club and waited for 5 mins went inside and no Tina, she got another taxi........to this day she has never let me forget it....and she still uses us !!

## Tim's Taxi Stories

"The Early days"
Back when we first started up "K Kabs" ( I even remember the number 849862) in the early 80's. We had an office at 3 Oxford Grove... we had started the company with 2 brown mark three cortinas, in those days to save money we use to do a lot of the car maintenance ourselves, my brother in law did most of it. One day we were

quite busy and the office was full of customers waiting for taxis.

My brother in-law was on the radio and was having a problem getting through to one of our drivers, this driver was a scouser who was as a liverpudlian never short of a few words.. all my brother in law could get was "having a problem with this car soft lad" My brother in law kept saying " please return to the office to pick up".. suddenly the driver burst into the office with a steering wheel in his hand.. "its come off" he says.. I don't know who was more shocked my brother in law or the customers who waiting for a taxi.

"The London Taxi"
After a few years of running "K Kabs" ,we took on drivers with their own vehicles. One driver decided to go up to London and buy a Proper London taxi cab. Brilliant and iconic vehicles around the streets of London and other cities, but not really designed for the hills and little streets of Ilfracombe. The driver got the taxi plated to carry 7 passengers, which was very popular with the youngsters on a Saturday night on the many runs down to the " Marisco Disco" down in Woolacombe. After a

while the poor old London cab was feeling the pace, it had done several hundred thousand miles even before it came to sunny Devon, and started to smoke a little, then as the summer season progressed it got worse and worse... my abiding memory of this was following the taxi up Mullacott on one its many trips down to Woolacombe, always full of the allotted passengers, if you didn't hear you were approaching it, you would see the smoke billowing out of the exhaust, as it crawled up the hill towards Mullacott cross roundabout. The taxi was always totally lost from view surrounded smoke, and you if couldn't hear the noise from the engine you would see a cloud of exhaust fumes coming towards you. Eventually the poor taxi went to the great taxi rank in the sky after just one summer in Ilfracombe.

RAF
Many years ago I picked up a serviceman from the rank to go to Chivenor, this was when it was a RAF base, and the security is not as it is now. When we got near the base the man asked if I could take him right on to the base, and he knew a short cut which would bypass the main gate....

before I knew it we were travelling down the main runway, suddenly I saw lights in my rear mirror, my first thought that it was a plane landing, but it was the RAF police who caught up with me and escorted me off the base with a flea in my ear... as for my passenger?, he was carted off by two burley RAF policeman, not before he had paid me his fare.

Food Order
I picked a food order from the Tandoori to go to Sandyway caravan site in Combe Martin, the curry was boxed up on my passenger seat, as I turned into the entrance on the caravan park a car was coming out of the entrance the wrong way, I braked to avoid the car, and the box flew off the front seat.... there was vindaloo up the dash, biriani on the floor and broken popadoms everywhere, I stopped and glanced down at the carnage as the recipient of the the curry opened the passenger door looked down on the floor and dashboard, and said "I'll pass on that mate" and closed the door. Not only had I lost the fare to Combe Martin, I had paid for the curry, and then lost valuable time cleaning up the mess. The moral of this story is never put a takeaway on the front seat !!!!

I was driving towards the Sandpiper Inn where there had been a big birthday party, a young lad flagged me down in St James Place, he was quite drunk,(no change there). "Braunton please Drive" he said. "Cost you £20 mate" I replied as it was gone midnight. He got in and off we went, he said he'd just had a big row with his girl friend. As we got into Braunton he said he had to get out to have a wee.. alarm bells ringing I get out of the taxi, he has his wee and starts to stagger off. … "Excuse me mate you haven't paid me" I tell him .. he turns round and tells me to f### off and he wasn't going to pay me, as he did two lads appeared around the corner one said asked me if I was alright ?? I said this idiot was refusing to pay his fare.

The one lad turns to my passenger as asks him to pay me as the driver is only trying to earn a living…..to which my passenger started to verbally abuse and threaten the one lad. Suddenly this lad lays into my passenger and a fight begins. This was time for me to make a swift exit, and put the saga down to experience..

I return to Ilfracombe minus the £20 as I enter the high street a girl flags me down by the

Welly pub, she jumps in and says "Can you take me to Braunton as quick as possible as my boyfriend has been beaten up"..... Off we go,…. I explain to her that it may be coincidence but I had just taken a lad to Braunton, and he refused to pay the fare, she described what he was wearing, and you've guessed it !!!…. it was him.. she apologises for him and insisted on stopping at the cash point to get me the £20 he owed me as well as the £20 for her fare. I dropped her outside the pixie stores, and she told me to wait and went Into her house then frogmarched the battered boyfriend out to apologise to me personally, and she demanded he gave me a tip, he gave me a fiver... I don't think he'll be doing that again in a hurry !!!

Rizlas
The phone rings, "can u pick me up a packet of rizla (ciggypapers) and bring them to The top of Oxford Grove". To which I reply "do you want several packets so you don't run out again" no he says just the one packet... 20p for the papers and £2.50 fare.. some people have too much money to burn….

(Food Orders)

The phone rings "hello Tim it's ######## can you pick a pizza up for me" "Of course we can" I replied "if you order it, let me know what time you want it picked up". "It's a Large Hawaiian extra crust and it will be ready in 20 minutes"…. no problem where is it being picked up from" ..... "its at the Pizza Ho in Barnstaple"....ahem I say "it's a £25 fare to Barnstaple."... "that's no problem I love their pizzas". So I send Callie off to pick up the most expensive pizza in North Devon. £13.50 for the pizza and £25 to deliver it..grand total £38.50………

Burger
One of the kebab shops rings up  "Hello my friend can you do a delivery for us please ?"… "I expect so, I reply" where is it going ? "It is going to Combe Martin how much will the delivery cost... "Combe Martin is £15 " I say "but it's only a cheese burger with extra relish which costs £6.50"......they did not have that burger delivered by taxi.

 "Rawhide"
I picked up a regular from the now closed The Conservative Club in Market Street. My passenger had a caravan up at Mullacott Park on the outskirts

of Ilfracombe. We proceeding up to Mullacott Cross when on a bend outside Mullacott Stables we were confronted by at least 20 horses in the road. I stopped with 2 other cars and got out of the taxi wondering what to do about the escaped horses, on the other side of the horses were some other cars, which had also stopped. As is was 2am in the morning the only thing I thought we could do was to herd the frightened animals back into stables.

I suggested that the three cars on the other side of the horses move slowly down to the entrance of the stables while we reversed back so all horses were trapped between the two rows of cars, we then moved slowly the three cars in a row and the horses were herded slowly into the entrance of the stables, each car having its window down we were waving out of the windows with imaginary lassos and shouting ye ha.. the horses went into the field, I got out and closed the open gate, to rapturous applause from from all the temporary cowboys.

Another incident ironically just up the road between the West Down turn off and Mullacott Cross. It was 4am in the morning when I was confronted by a herd of escaped cows. For 10 minutes they just stood there staring at me in the taxi, I moved forward very slowly and at one stage I thought they weren't going to move suddenly they about turned and started to leg it back along the road to the field, I again herded them into the field, no lassos or ye ha were needed as I closed them back in the field, this time too no applause.

"What a coincidence"

A few years ago (it must of been a long time ago because taxi meters hadn't been introduced) I was flagged down by the Britannia Hotel on the seafront by two gentlemen "can you take us to the Gloucester ??"…. "no problem" I replied and started off to go the other side of the seafront... "how much is that going to cost us??" an inquiry from back seat, "to the Gloucester hotel about 60p" "No" he said,…. "we want to go to Gloucester"…… "What Dr Foster went to Gloucester Gloucester" I replied. "Yes" was the response. I worked out a price and off we went. I told them that my Father lived in Gloucester, "where?? " they asked I told them and they laughed as they wanted to be dropped in the next street.. unfortunately, it was gone 2am by the time I got there, so I couldn't visit my father.

Another time two very drunk Welsh lads missed the ferry back to Swansea (a very common occurrence as they couldn't cope with the Devon beer and ciders)... they had to get back to Penarth in South Wales, which was where I was born and where my grandmother lived, again because I got there in the early hours of the morning, I couldn't visit her. Both my grandmother and father said I should of visited them but at the time I didn't think it was a good idea.

Thinking back to those days where the 4 lads got the money for the two taxi's because they both had the cash…..as this was before ATMs and I'm sure both taxi's took place on a Sunday when the banks were closed.

The Marisco Disco

To those who don't know the Marisco Club is the country's longest running night club, I believe it been running since the 1970s. It is located in Woolacombe (which just recently was voted to have the best beach in the country) 5 miles from Ilfracombe, every Saturday night in the 80s there would be a mass exodus from Ilfracombe down to the Marisco. In those days the fare was around £6 return (now it is about £35 return) the fares were always paid up front and we'd spend all Saturday evenings taking people down there, if you did 10 trips down there you would do 10 return trips when the Marisco closed at 2pm. The funny thing was you never brought the same people back , as long as everyone did the same number of trips down there everyone got home.


" Lost Again"
A guy in Woolacombe asked if I could do a run up to Frinton on Sea, which is up on the east coast, it was to take loads of women's clothes up as he ran a mail order business, to help with the cost of this journey would I drop his father in-law into the centre of London. We negotiated a price as the clothes had to be up in Frinton on Sea buy the end of the next day. I arrived in Woolacombe the next day nice and early to be confronted with about 20 boxes of these clothes, No way could I get all these boxes and the father in law in the taxi, which was a mark 3 Cortina (shows how long ago it was).
            The guy said that the boxes weren't that important and could we put the clothes loose in the boot and back of the car, the boot and back seat were absolutely full to the roof with various ladies clothes. I asked where in London we were

going ??? ….don't worry my father in law is a cockney born and bred and knows London like the back of his hand. The journey was uneventful up to the smoke, what the gentleman had forgotten to tell me he had moved away from London 30 years earlier, he says to me "don't worry son, I know all the back streets" after an couple of hours of "go down this road" ...."turn right here" and "where's that pub gone" we were totally lost, my A to Z of London was as much use as a chocolate fireguard. Trying to ask people for directions wasn't helping much either don't know if it was my accent or the people I asked didn't speak English.

Eventually I found someone who could help us, as she started to tell us some directions the clothes in the back seat tipped forward and my passenger ended up with a ladies bra on his head wearing them like a set of ear muffs. The lady took one look at my passenger stopped then backed away …end of conversation. We eventually found our address thanks to the help of a black cab. I managed to drop the clothes off to Frinton on Sea without any more dramas.

"Lundy Island"

Last summer Gaynor our controller sent me down to the Pier, to pick up off the Oldenburg the Lundy Island Ferry. She told me there were six passengers wanting to go to the Imperial Hotel in Barnstaple. I was in the Zafira which was a six seater, the one thing that bothered me on my way down to the pier was the absence of any mention of luggage... the fleet mini bus was out on another job, so I arrived by the Lundy booking office where there were 6 people waiting, with the biggest pile of luggage I'd seen since my wife last went on holiday.

The passengers looked at the taxi and then looked at the luggage, right I said "this might be interesting" two lads got in the rear seats and said to pile the luggage on top of them, I managed to put some bags in the back ,then piled as instructed some more on top of the two lads, all that could be seen were two sets of eyes peeking out between the mountain of luggage. Three more in the middle seats again pile the luggage on top nearly up to the roof of the car. Finally a chap sat in front again with luggage up to his chin.

Having some how getting the mountain luggage plus the passengers on board we were off to Barnstaple.

Anyone who saw us must of thought I had a taxi full of luggage as they couldn't see any passengers. The 20 minute journey everyone in the taxi was laughing as they could not see out the the mound of luggage. Luckily I was the only one who see where we were going, which was fortunate, as I was driving.

We got to Barnstaple safely and managed to get first the luggage then 6 very squashed passengers. They thanked me for the most exciting taxi ride ever and gave a nice tip.

"More food orders"

A gentleman rang me and asked if I was willing to pick a food order up and take it to Lee Bay, It was quite a large order, if fact it was nearly £200 worth. He gave me his phone number and the address and some directions as the house wasn't easy to find, alarm bells should of rang but my ego kicked in and I said I knew where every place was, where really I hadn't got a clue.

Lee Bay is a little village 2 miles west of Ilfracombe and is famous for having the 70s series Smugglers starring Oliver Tobias filmed there. It contains a lot  of holiday homes and can be like a ghost town off season.

I followed the man's instructions but every house I went past was in darkness, after 20 min of driving around, I had no phone signal, I thought that all the taxi drivers were going to have a great meal on me, I decided to go back towards Ilfracombe where I would get a phone signal. I rang the number ... no answer

I was now beginning to panic, as the banquet of Chinese was now getting cold, suddenly as I contemplated feeding all the taxi drivers in Ilfracombe, the phone rang it was that gentleman who was on a landline and had given me the wrong directions, he said he would walk down to the main road, I found him and he showed me the way to go suddenly out of the darkness there was light and 20 hungry people cheering as appeared with their food. He paid for the food and the fare and £20 tip for my trouble.

Merry Christmas
One of the takeaways rang and asked could I do a delivery to Torres Park in an hour. I arrived on the hour to be confronted with two big boxes on the counter, the order cost £145 and was going to a hotel on Torres park. I carried the boxes down to the entrance and rang the bell and a lady arrived,

and proceeded to count out £145 and gave it too me, "there is the taxi fare as well please " I told her . "I shouldn't have to pay that" she said grumpily... started to argue about the fare but begrudging gave me the taxi fare ... then slammed the door in my face as I wished her Merry Christmas.

I took the monies back to the takeaway and told them what had occurred. They said they had said they didn't do deliveries but could send it down in a taxi, to which she agreed. Some people are full of the festive cheer!!!


"Wounded in action"

One Friday 13th.. and it was unlucky for me..I picked up the phone from Colin the boss at the the start of my shift he said my first fare was a six seater job from the seafront to Chambercombe.

I arrived at the pickup to be confronted by two boys with a big bike. I put the back seats down.. and lifted the bike into the back of the taxi the handle bars swing back and catch me in the right eye.. I see stars for a moment.. but as the soldier I am, I don't complain.. I arrive at Chambercombe and proceed to remove the bike from the back seats. This time the bike gets caught in the seat belt and swings back and catches me in the left eye..... I curse quietly and give the bike to one of the two lads, both eyes are stinging now finish the week end looking like Chi Chi the giant panda....

"How Much !!!!"
It was the early hours of a Sunday morning, I was number one on the rank, a man staggers round the corner, Oxford grove rank is situated on a very steep road, so with this gentleman it was two steps forward then one step backwards. He eventually gets to my taxi and I wind the passenger window down, " how much to Braunton mate??" he asks…. about £30 "I reply..."bloody hell" he says…. I need some more cash, with this he about turns and staggers down to the Barclays Bank ATM which is situated fortunately for us taxi drivers right at the bottom of the rank… 5 min later he gets into my taxi and gives me the £30. And off we go.

The journey to Braunton takes about 15mins , the whole duration of this journey the man complains about the price of the fare. It was why was it so much??.. how much fuel does the taxi actually use??, who sets the prices??, who can I complain to about the price.. I tell him to contact the North Devon Council....who set the fares.. I have the meter on for the duration of the journey... we get to Braunton and the meter reads £32.50... he gets out of the taxi then proceeds to give me a £10 tip ......weird or what !!!!

" How come you know where I live"

Again a bloke staggers round the corner of the rank, he was completely out of it. He gets in and says "Braunton please" (as per last story the People of Braunton are right pissheads).. we get to Braunton and he directs me right to his front door pays me the fare says good night.. and off I go back to Ilfracombe.

A week later the same man walks round the corner this time he isn't totally sober but he gets in the taxi and before he could say anything I say "Braunton yes ??".. he looks at me and says " how do you know that ??".. I reply " I took you home last week"..... " no you didn't, I would remember". I explain that I did and I would take him right to his front door... the journey to Braunton he was very quiet, still not believing that I knew where he lived.. I dropped him at his front door.. he paid me and gave me that look that he still didn't believe that I had taken him home the previous week.

" The kebab" ( not for the Squeamish)

I had gone home for a quick cup of tea, and to see the wife, having had my tea break I got back into the taxi I was met with the smell of a kebab. I looked into the back seat to find a very sad looking kebab on the floor.
I picked it up and decided to put it in the waste bin opposite, unfortunately for me I had the car keys in the same hand and the kebab and keys went straight into the waste bin. It was one of the waste bins with two little openings on the side to put your rubbish in. After several expletives, I had to get onto my knees and just managed to get my arm into the bin to attempt to retrieve the set of car keys. The bin was nearly full, with all sorts of gooey substances including the very sad looking kebab.

After several minutes of feeling about in the quagmire, no keys !!. By this time people were walking past looking at me and must of thought this taxi driver must of hit hard times cause he was raiding the waste bin. I explained several times what had happened, I'm sure some of them didn't believe me. The only thing I could do was to empty the bin by hand, I dashed home and got a black bag, and proceeded to empty the contents of the bin by hand into the black bag, it was that Rodney Trotter moment when he was trying to retrieve Biffo's trumpet from the waste Shute in that Fools and Horses episode... there were all sorts of unspeakable bits in the bin and it stunk to high heaven, having nearly emptied the whole bin into the black bag and still no keys, I was now down to the near liquid contents in the bottom of the bin if you get my jest, after several attempts of pulling out several unsavoury items.. bingo my fingers found the keys and I pulled them out, with whoops of joy as I held the keys above my head like I was displaying winning the FA cup. What the passerby must of thought I have know idea....

I was working with Ricky one night and told him to go and pick up at the Bunch of Grapes going

to Berrynarbour, he waited outside……
nothing……..drunken guy tries to get in his taxi
and he had to push him out and close the
door…..still nothing……he waited 7 mins then
pulled away, in the mean time this girl calls me
and asked where her taxi was ??….I told her that
Ricky was waiting outside the Bunch of Grapes
for over 5 mins…….she says she's not there……
she is at Chickenland around the corner…..I said
how on earth are we suppose to know
that !!!!!!…..anyway Ricky came back and
picked them up and took them to Berrynarbour.

Well, that's all folks, we hope you all enjoyed
our stories and some at the time were very funny
for us and we are both glad we had chance to
share them with you.
As you can see Ilfracombe has a lot of humorous
people and a great taxi service, who knows, one
day you might have a taxi with us and have a
story for us to tell.

Ricky & Tim

Printed in Great Britain
by Amazon